for Beatrice and Theo

Simon Paisley Day

RAVING

OBERON BOOKS
LONDON

WWW.OBERONBOOKS.COM

First published in 2013 by Oberon Books Ltd
521 Caledonian Road, London N7 9RH
Tel: +44 (0) 20 7607 3637 / Fax: +44 (0) 20 7607 3629
e-mail: info@oberonbooks.com
www.oberonbooks.com

A catalogue record for this book is available from the British Library.

PB ISBN: 978-1-78319-046-1
E ISBN: 978-1-78319-545-9

Cover photography by Shaun Webb
Cover design by SWD

Characters

BRIONY
40s, primary school teacher

KEITH
40s, secondary school teacher

SERENA
40s, doctor

CHARLES
40s, ex-army officer

ROSS
40s, PR consultant

ROSY
40s, PR consultant

TABBY
17, Serena's niece

MR. MORGAN
60s, farmer

*The action all takes place in a converted barn
on a remote Welsh hillside. Present day.*

Raving was first performed on 17 October 2013 at Hampstead Theatre with the following cast:

BRIONY	Tamzin Outhwaite
KEITH	Barnaby Kay
SERENA	Issy van Randwyck
CHARLES	Nicholas Rowe
ROSS	Robert Webb
ROSY	Sarah Hadland
TABBY	Bel Powley
MR MORGAN	Ifan Huw Dafydd

Writer	Simon Paisley Day
Director	Edward Hall
Designer	Jonathan Fensom
Lighting	Rick Fisher
Sound	Matt Mckenzie
Composer	Simon Slater
Casting	Cara Beckinsale CDG

Act One

Lights up on BRIONY standing in the centre of the main living-space. There is a sitting area, a dining table and chairs, and a kitchen area. The front door is clearly visible, as are three other doors leading to offstage bedrooms. BRIONY is holding her breasts, and looking clearly distressed as she takes in her environment. Two bags stand by the door, which stands open. She briefly looks in all the bedrooms. Enter KEITH through the front door.

BRIONY: Well? *(KEITH shakes his head.)* I don't believe it. You looked everywhere? Under the seats? Glove compartment?

KEITH: Everywhere. I took it apart.

BRIONY: You had it when we left London. It must have fallen out of your pocket.

KEITH: When?

BRIONY: At that service station. We're in the middle of nowhere, Keith. Why does this sort of thing always happen to us?

KEITH: It doesn't.

BRIONY: Can you imagine Ross and Rosy ever losing anything? They wouldn't.

KEITH: Good for them.

BRIONY: Yes, and bad for us. It makes me feel like a total failure.

KEITH: It's only a phone.

BRIONY: No, it's a lifeline. We're on a Welsh bloody hillside, two hundred miles from our son.

KEITH: It's about one seventy, actually. But yeah, you're right.

BRIONY: Why doesn't she get her own bloody phone?

KEITH: Who?

BRIONY: Your mum. If she had her own phone she wouldn't have had to borrow mine. And we wouldn't now be stranded.

KEITH: The others will be here soon. We'll call from one of theirs.

BRIONY: What if they're not though? What if no one comes? My boobs are killing me. If you forgot the breast-pump I'm going to…

KEITH: It's here.

He takes various bits of plastic from a bag and begins to fit them together.

BRIONY: I'll do it.

Over the next section BRIONY fits the breast-pump and expresses milk into it.

KEITH: Nice place.

BRIONY: Very Welsh.

KEITH: Nice though.

BRIONY: Course it is. Ross organised it. I sometimes wonder how on earth people as pathetic as you and me are allowed to start a family. It's far more dangerous than driving a car, yet there's not a single test, nothing. I was thinking that on the M4. Any old idiot can just drive straight onto the six-lane motorway, dodging the juggernauts, causing great huge pile-ups in their wake. Bodies and blood all over the tarmac.

KEITH: They're not meant to. Not without green L-plates. So other drivers…

BRIONY: I'm talking about parenthood, Keith. The six-lane highway of psychological carnage.

KEITH: I think we're doing all right.

BRIONY: Do you?

KEITH: Yes.

Pause.

BRIONY: I still can't believe we're the first ones here.

KEITH: Maybe we're not quite as pathetic as you think.

BRIONY: We're probably in the wrong house. Are you sure he said Wales, not Scotland? The front door wasn't locked. This is probably the farmer's house. He's going to come in any second now and blow our brains out with a shotgun for trespassing. For being English.

KEITH: I thought you didn't do stereotypes.

BRIONY: You've restored my faith in them. Maybe he'll let us make one final call to Finn before he puts us out of our misery.

KEITH: I'll boil some water.

He goes into the kitchen area and fills the kettle.

BRIONY: 'Hello darling. Just wanted to let you know we love you. Have a nice life with Granny and Gramps. We'd only have messed you up.'

KEITH: There must be some teabags.

BRIONY: 'Oh, and Finn, one little tip: never, ever come to Wales.' Bang. The end. London couple in weekend break tragedy. What?

KEITH: Nothing.

BRIONY: I know that look.

KEITH: I just think you're still…

BRIONY: No, I'm not.

KEITH: Fine.

BRIONY: I'm not. I don't need them. *(Pause.)* And they've got a Beamer.

KEITH: What?

BRIONY: A Beamer. Ross and Rosy. Top of the range. I don't understand why they're not here. We didn't see any smash-ups, did we? At least little Rollo and Hebe aren't involved.

KEITH: Briony…

BRIONY: They always say that, don't they? But it depends on the extent of the injuries. I mean, what sort of life are they condemned to if Ross and Rosy are killed, or left as vegetables? They're all better off dying.

KEITH: Jesus.

BRIONY: With us though, I seriously think Finn's life wouldn't be that much worse with his grandparents.

KEITH: I really think you're…

BRIONY: I'm just saying, it's weird. That they're not here. Given how much they like to…you know.

KEITH: What?

BRIONY: Oh come on. You've known Ross for years. Was he like that at school?

KEITH: Like what?

BRIONY: Controlling.

KEITH: Well, yes, but…

BRIONY: They're both as bad as each other. The batch-freezing, the routines, the lack of any mess, never a single magazine out of place, her perfect hair and teeth, his ties. They don't do late. There's no room in their lives for the chaos that lateness brings. Everything's controlled with surgical precision. Finances, parenting – their perfect children and their perfect manners. They've even trained them to tidy away their toys. Have you ever seen them drink too much? God knows, it might lead to an argument. But in fact there's nothing to argue about. Any potential cause of disquiet is stifled in early infancy. Managed, disappeared. The science lab of marital bliss in happy nappy valley.

KEITH: Wow.

BRIONY: What?

KEITH: We're going back to London. You need your pills.

BRIONY: They're just thoughts. I don't care how they live their lives.

She unscrews the bottle from the pump and holds it out to him. He takes it.

Take this, will you? I'm not threatened by what they've got.

KEITH: I didn't say you were.

BRIONY: Live and let live. That's my motto.

(KEITH heads off towards a bedroom.)

Where are you going?

KEITH: To flush it.

BRIONY: Flush it?

KEITH: Yes?

BRIONY: Down the toilet?

KEITH: Well, you don't want to keep it, do you?

BRIONY: It's my milk, Keith.

KEITH: I know.

BRIONY: Don't flush my milk down the toilet. It's not urine.

KEITH: Obviously.

BRIONY: The toilet is where we discard our waste products.

KEITH: Yes, I know that.

BRIONY: Vomit. Faeces, Keith. This is different. This is nourishment for our child. It's liquid love.

KEITH: Right.

BRIONY: I'm amazed you'd even think of flushing it.

KEITH: Sorry. I didn't…

BRIONY: Use the sink.

KEITH: Okay.

He goes over to the kitchen, but instead of pouring it down the sink he puts a lid on it and stows it in a drawer, unseen by BRIONY. He washes the pump.

BRIONY: They're basically all right though.

KEITH: What?

BRIONY: Ross and Rosy. They're not bad people. Ambitious, yes, sometimes judgmental and patronising, but all right. As opposed to some of their friends who are just plain vile. Like Serena and Charles.

KEITH: Vile?

BRIONY: Can you imagine? Not that they would, but if Serena suddenly said 'we're organising a weekend away and we'd love you to come'…

KEITH: God.

BRIONY: *(Laughs.)* Imagine, Keith.

KEITH: I am. Christ.

BRIONY: Of course they'd only do it to humiliate us.

KEITH: Well…

BRIONY: Charles would say 'ya, it's this amazing rectory from the 58th century BC' and then when we got there we'd find there'd been a frightful mix-up and we weren't invited at all, on account of insufficient breeding, or money…

KEITH: I don't think…

BRIONY: Definitely.

KEITH: But we've hardly even spent any…

BRIONY: I don't need to. I can tell, Keith. They're rude. And weird. And snobby. Rinse it properly, will you?

(He rinses it again and puts it away.)

Snooty bastards. And they bring out a very unlikeable side to Ross and Rosy.

KEITH: Do you like anyone?

BRIONY: What's that supposed to mean?

KEITH: I just wonder sometimes whether you actually like anyone.

BRIONY: What a terrible thing to say. Of course I do. I like Ross and Rosy. Why else would I agree to spend three whole days with them? And I love Danni and Phil. Thank

God they're coming. Danni and Phil are normal. Of course I like people. And I don't need my pills. I'm going to choose a room. What?

KEITH: Nothing.

BRIONY: First come, first served. There's no pecking order.

KEITH: I just think it's polite, since Ross and Rosy have, you know, organised everything...bought all the food...

BRIONY: Right. No, of course. God, I'm so selfish.

KEITH: No, you're not.

BRIONY: I am. You're so much more...

KEITH: No, I'm not.

BRIONY: You are. You think about others. You're a wonderful man, and the best father Finn could ever have had. *(Tearful.)* The best partner too.

KEITH: Oh come on.

BRIONY: Will you promise me something?

KEITH: What?

BRIONY: If anything awful happens this weekend...

KEITH: Oh for heaven's sake.

BRIONY: But if it does.

KEITH: It won't.

BRIONY: But if it does, promise me you'll look after Finn.

KEITH: Briony.

BRIONY: Promise me.

KEITH: I promise. Now try and relax. That's why we're here. We thought it might help, didn't we?

KEITH holds her.

BRIONY: Do my neck.

(KEITH gently massages her neck and shoulders.)

That's good. Who'll tell their children, Keith? If they have been killed in some horrific accident? We'll have to.

KEITH: They're fine. They've broken down somewhere. Relax.

BRIONY: You've got healing hands, Keithy. I don't know what I'd do without you. I love you.

KEITH: I love you too.

He massages more decidedly.

BRIONY: Mmmmm. That's good.

KEITH: Is it?

BRIONY: Yes.

KEITH: I love you so much.

BRIONY: Mmmmmmmm.

(He leans in and starts to kiss her neck. She stiffens. He continues.)

Why do you always do that?

KEITH: I don't.

BRIONY: Why does it always have to be a kind of foreplay? I'm very tense at the moment.

KEITH: I know.

BRIONY: And that sort of pressure really doesn't help. I'm not ready. I've told you this before.

KEITH: It's just that it's been…

BRIONY: I know. I'm failing you as a wife. Like I'm failing Finn as a mother.

KEITH: Christ.

BRIONY: I'd have an affair if I were you. With your French assistant. She'll give you what you need. I want to speak to my child. I miss him. I don't know why we came here!

KEITH: Where are you going?

BRIONY: To the toilet. I need to be alone.

She exits to one of the bedrooms. Exasperated, KEITH collapses on the sofa. Headlights are seen outside. He leaps up. He calls to BRIONY.

KEITH: Someone's here!

(He looks out of the window.)

What the…? Briony! Briony!

BRIONY: *(Off.)* What?

KEITH: Come here!

BRIONY: *(Off.)* Why?

KEITH: Now, Briony!

BRIONY: Hang on!

KEITH: No! No, no, no, no, no! I don't believe it. Briony! Quickly!

Flushing offstage. BRIONY re-enters.

BRIONY: What is it?

KEITH: They're here.

BRIONY: Oh. Thank God.

KEITH: Charles and Serena.

BRIONY: What?

KEITH: Charles and Serena. I don't understand.

BRIONY: What are they doing here?

KEITH: I don't know.

BRIONY: They can't be here.

KEITH: They are.

BRIONY: But this is our first weekend away ever. They can't ruin it!

KEITH: Get it together, Briony.

The door opens and CHARLES and SERENA enter, with a box of chocolates and a bottle of whisky.

SERENA: What an absolute fucker of a journey. I mean, I ask you, what is the point of coming so far away from the Metrop? What the hell is wrong with the Cotswolds? Have you been here for hours?

BRIONY: Not really. We…

SERENA: Where are Ross and Rosy?

KEITH: Not here.

SERENA: I know that. I mean, unless they came on foot.

CHARLES laughs uproariously at this. He opens the whisky and hunts for glasses.

CHARLES: I like that. On foot! With all the shopping!

SERENA: Haven't they rung?

BRIONY: I don't know. We lost our phone.

SERENA: Oh, hard luck. I always do that. I get through about one a week.

KEITH: I wonder if we could use yours. Just to ring home.

SERENA: Chas.

CHARLES: What?

SERENA: They need your phone.

CHARLES: Oh right.

CHARLES gives KEITH his phone.

SERENA: You probably didn't even know we were coming. The other two dropped out.

CHARLES: Fanny and Dill.

BRIONY: Danni and Phil.

SERENA: They got a better offer. Not really. Their kid went down with a fever this morning so Ross asked us if we fancied a weekend away.

BRIONY: Poor little Riley.

CHARLES: But he told us not to tell you. In case you cancelled as well.

BRIONY: Why would we do that?

SERENA: Exactly.

BRIONY: We're very fond of you, aren't we Keith?

KEITH: What?

BRIONY: Really fond. Aren't we?

KEITH: Yes. Really fond.

BRIONY: Not that we know you all that well, but…

CHARLES: No, not because we were coming. He told us not to tell you because you'd started worrying about your little… wotsit.

BRIONY: Finn.

CHARLES: That's it.

SERENA: But he's fine, isn't he?

BRIONY: Yes, I think so…

SERENA: Of course he is. Kids are so resilient.

KEITH: There's no bloody connection.

SERENA: Well, if you're patient, I'll explain.

KEITH: No, I mean the…

SERENA: You see, Ross said he thought they'd had a play date recently…

BRIONY: Oh, I see. Well, yes, they were going to, but Finn was naughty so…

KEITH: There's no signal.

BRIONY: I didn't handle it very well, really. We went to the health food shop together and Finn kept pointing at this tub of black olives that he said looked like…you know…

SERENA: Poos?

BRIONY: Yes. And he kept doing it, and the more I tried to get him to stop, the more he did it, pointing at the olives and saying 'look, Mummy, little black poopoos, little smelly poopoos'. It was awful. So then I threatened him with cancelling his play date with Riley and that's when he completely lost it. Kicking, screaming, throwing the olives at me – and the other customers. I had to walk out.

SERENA: Fucking nightmare.

BRIONY: So he didn't go to Riley's house, but he said he didn't care. And I was the one who walked out of the shop. I lost the battle. I'm not really cut out for motherhood.

KEITH: I'll try outside. He said there'd be coverage.

CHARLES: What?

KEITH: Ross said there'd be coverage on all networks. But there's nothing.

KEITH exits.

BRIONY: What would you have done?

SERENA: I'd have let him carry on calling them poopoos.

CHARLES: Or worse.

SERENA: We're dreadful.

CHARLES: She'd probably have joined in.

BRIONY: Does that work? I don't see how it can.

SERENA: No, but it makes life so much more fun.

CHARLES: We love a good food fight.

SERENA: They're going to turn out exactly how they turn out regardless of what we do to them, so let them get on with it, I say.

BRIONY: I try doing that sometimes, but it doesn't seem to work. I've read so many different books and they all say different things.

CHARLES: Have to be consistent. Kids are like dogs – slightly less fun, slightly less useful – but you can't afford to confuse them. That's when they turn nasty. Decide on your training program and stick to it.

BRIONY: But Finn's three now.

CHARLES: Oh well, you're buggered then.

KEITH re-enters.

KEITH: I don't believe it.

CHARLES: What?

KEITH: No bars. Not a single bloody bar.

CHARLES: That's because it's dairy.

KEITH: What?

CHARLES: You don't get sheep on a dairy farm. Plenty of moos, no baahs. How are you getting on with the phone?

KEITH: I was talking about the phone.

CHARLES: I know.

CHARLES finds this hilarious.

BRIONY: Did he really ask you not to tell us?

SERENA: Not a single baah!

KEITH: That's right.

CHARLES: Only moos!

BRIONY: Serena.

SERENA: What?

BRIONY: Did Ross really tell you not to tell us?

SERENA: Yes, but honestly, he truly thinks you need this break. And you do, don't you? You look shattered.

BRIONY: Thanks.

SERENA: I mean, you're back full-time now, aren't you?

BRIONY: I went back when Finn was one and a half.

SERENA: Oh. Of course.

CHARLES: I say old man, fancy giving me a hand with the bags?

KEITH: Um…all right.

CHARLES: Something I want to show you.

They exit.

SERENA: They must have broken down somewhere, I suppose. It's social work, isn't it?

BRIONY: What?

SERENA: What you do.

BRIONY: I teach reception.

SERENA: Exactly.

BRIONY: It's pretty exhausting. I'd love not to work at all, but Keith's a teacher too, as you know, so... It must be wonderful. Not working.

SERENA: I suppose.

BRIONY: Is it?

SERENA: I don't know.

BRIONY: But I thought... I didn't think you...do you work?

SERENA: After a fashion.

BRIONY: What do you do?

SERENA: I'm a doctor.

BRIONY: A doctor?

SERENA: Yes.

BRIONY: What sort of doctor?

SERENA: Oh...

BRIONY: You've never mentioned...

SERENA: I never talk about work. Unless it's something really funny like an exploding stomach or a hoover attachment that won't come off...

BRIONY: I really thought you were a lady of leisure.

SERENA: Oh I could be, but I'd go loopy. It's a hobby, really. Fills the gap.

BRIONY: And saves lives.

SERENA: Yes, that too.

CHARLES and KEITH re-enter, carrying cases – and a gun, in its special bag.

CHARLES: I'll go and talk to the farmer about it. They're always pretty keen. As long as you don't hit the bloody cows. Wants to learn to shoot.

BRIONY: Keith?

KEITH: I didn't…

SERENA: He's a damned good teacher. Trained with the SAS.

KEITH: I didn't actually say…

CHARLES: We'll start with vermin: rats, rabbits, ex-coal miners…

SERENA: Charlie.

CHARLES: Might even bag ourselves a pheasant.

BRIONY: We don't like guns. We used to be hunt saboteurs. It's something we care a lot about.

CHARLES: Oh that's all right. Each to his own, I say.

BRIONY: Would you keep the gun in your car please? I'm sorry.

KEITH: I'm sure he'll…

BRIONY: Please.

SERENA: Of course. Chas. Shooter. Back in the car.

CHARLES: Oh. Right-oh.

SERENA: I'll put these in the room. Is this one taken?

She takes the bags and heads towards one of the bedrooms.

BRIONY: Er…we were going to…

SERENA: *(Off.)* Fuck! It's lovely and big.

CHARLES: Sorry about the old girl. Mouth like a bleeding navvy.

SERENA: *(Off.)* Oh, and there's a fucking adorable little bathroom.

He exits with the gun. BRIONY takes their bags and goes towards the second biggest room.

KEITH: Briony.

BRIONY: Well I don't see why we should have to have the smallest room.

(But she stops.)

I don't want you touching that gun.

KEITH: I won't.

She takes the bags into the bedroom. KEITH has a moment. BRIONY re-emerges.

BRIONY: He was all right, wasn't he?

KEITH: Who?

BRIONY: Finn. When we left.

KEITH: He was fine.

BRIONY: I miss him. I love him so much, even when he screams at me, even when I never want to see him again.

KEITH: That's why we're here. So we can learn to miss him a bit.

BRIONY: What happened with the phone?

KEITH: There was no reception.

BRIONY: What?

KEITH: I told you. No one ever listens to anything I say.

(Storming into the bedroom for the bags and taking them to the third bedroom.)

There are no bars! We can't speak to Finn. Ross obviously got it wrong when he said the phones would work, or perhaps he's with a better network. Better car, better job, better children!

BRIONY: Don't shout at me, please.

KEITH: I didn't…oh Christ!

She has exited to the third bedroom. SERENA returns.

SERENA: Where's Chas?

KEITH: I don't know.

SERENA: I'm starving. Is he still outside?

KEITH: I don't know. Yes, he is. Sorry.

He goes to the bedroom. SERENA begins looking through the kitchen cupboards.

SERENA: Ah. Here we are.

(She finds a tin of tomato soup, some cornflakes and a bag of raisins…)

Knew there'd be something.

BRIONY: *(Off.)* It's fine.

KEITH: *(Off.)* But we can easily…

BRIONY: *(Off.)* It's fine!

KEITH: *(Off.)* I'm sure they wouldn't mind…

BRIONY: *(Off.)* Please, just leave me alone!

KEITH re-enters, trying to put a brave face on things…

SERENA: Drink?

KEITH: No thanks. She's just…hungry. So am I.

SERENA: We're having polenta with a warm tomato coulis.

KEITH: Polenta?

SERENA: Golden flakes of corn. Just add water, mash it up, bake on a low heat. And this might look like bog-standard tomato soup but chuck in some of these…

KEITH: Raisins?

SERENA: Give it texture. Trust me, we know about survival. My granny used to eat grass and slugs.

KEITH: In the war?

SERENA: No, just mad, but she did live to a hundred and three. The human body is an extraordinary thing. Our little buggers eat what they want. Stones, lego. There's a lot of fibre in lego. Wholemeal lego anyway. Where the fuck is Charlie?

KEITH: Maybe he went off to kill something.

SERENA: He hasn't pissed you off, has he? He's such an insensitive git. Loves having a go at you lefties. Doesn't mean a word of it. He just thinks you're all a bunch of queers. He didn't say that to you, did he?

KEITH: No.

SERENA: Thank God. Yes, do-gooding, spineless queers. That's the line he normally comes out with. Outrageous really.

KEITH: I just don't really like guns.

SERENA: Don't be such a girl. It's fantastic. Cocking it, feeling it smash into your shoulder. And it's a damned sight fairer than buying a bloody chicken. At least they have a sporting chance when you hunt 'em.

KEITH: We always…the free-range organic chickens that we…

CHARLES returns, holding up a brace of partridge.

CHARLES: Supper!

SERENA: Oh you clever old bastard. What are they?

CHARLES: Partridge.

SERENA: How many shots?

CHARLES: I stalked them. Much more fun. You inch through the long grass till you're only a few yards away. Then you wait. Psych the buggers out. Then, suddenly, you go 'RAAAGH!' and they break cover. That's when you leap up and grab the fuckers by the neck. One in each hand. Smack their heads together.

SERENA: That's the SAS for you. Kiss me.

CHARLES: And if they're still not here by the morning I'll go and kill a cow.

SERENA: Shoot it?

CHARLES: Christ no. Make it look like a puma attack. Score the hide. Rip open the belly. Few teethmarks. Leave most of it in the field. We'd only want five or six kilos. It's actually great fun.

He finds a bin-liner under the sink and settles down to begin plucking the birds.

KEITH: I'm just going to…

SERENA: She in the bath?

KEITH: No. We haven't got a bath in our room.

SERENA: Shower?

KEITH: It doesn't really work properly. It's more of a dribble than a shower.

SERENA: Tell her to use ours.

KEITH: She's sort of having a splash in the...over the...bidet.

CHARLES: Aye aye.

KEITH: What?

CHARLES: Aye aye.

KEITH: Is something wrong?

CHARLES: Doesn't sound like it. If she's freshening up. Eh?

KEITH: No, the showerhead's not working. The bit at the end. It keeps sort of flopping.

CHARLES: *(Smiling.)* Ah.

KEITH: What? I'm trying to explain. The pipe that feeds into the end is too thin. There's no way you'd get any sort of gush even if the end didn't droop, which it does. It's a dribble, as I said.

CHARLES: Her brother had similar trouble. Spent half his inheritance on quack bloody remedies. This was way before Viagra. He was up and down Harley Street, tried all the creams and pills, magazines, high-class hookers, forking out a fortune and never once getting old Percy out of his Parker Knoll.

SERENA: And then you took him hunting.

CHARLES: He'd never been. Cured him. First thing he killed. Up it went. Ping. It's not sporting prowess or anything like that. It's killing something. Reaffirms you. Makes you whole again. Proper.

SERENA: Boner fide.

CHARLES: Brilliant. Boner fide. Boner fucking fide. Brilliant. *(He laughs uproariously.)*

KEITH: We don't actually have a... I'm not...

CHARLES: Boner fide!

KEITH: I was actually talking about…

CHARLES: Don't worry. I'll get you out tomorrow. Bang bang! Get it? Bang! Bang! Get things working again. Boner fide. Fucking brilliant.

(BRIONY enters.)

Shhh. Mum's the word.

BRIONY: What about?

SERENA: Nothing.

CHARLES: Don't want to spoil the surprise. Should be worth waiting for. Ping ping.

SERENA: Supper's all sorted.

BRIONY: If you're talking about those birds you killed, I saw you coming back with them, and I'm happy to go without.

SERENA: Don't worry. There'll be plenty polenta.

BRIONY sits in an armchair.

CHARLES: *(Sotto voce.)* You wait and see old man. Tomorrow. *(Mimes shooting.)*

BRIONY: *(Seeing the bin-liner and the birds.)* Oh God!

SERENA: Go and pluck those outside, will you? Go on. Pluck off out of it.

CHARLES finds this very amusing. He takes the partridges and exits.

BRIONY: We should try and speak to Ross and Rosy. Someone should drive down to the farmer's house. I'm sure he'd let us use his landline. He must have a landline. That way we know where we stand. I mean, if they're involved in a hideous crash or something…

SERENA: Then at least we'll be sure the food's not coming and we can keep the partridge back for breakfast…

BRIONY: No. I mean…it's the not knowing. I just don't understand why they're not here.

SERENA: Maybe they had no intention of coming whatsoever. Maybe they decided the four of us all needed to spend some quality time together. Thrown into the wild, like one of those ghastly reality TV things. Would they rip each other apart? Or would they end up swapping partners in a steamy four-way love-in?

(Uncomfortable beat.)

Joke.

An excited CHARLES re-enters with the semi-plucked partridges.

CHARLES: They're here!

SERENA: Hoorah! Which one's Ross and which one's Rosy?

CHARLES: No. They're coming up the lane.

BRIONY: Oh thank God.

KEITH: Finally!

SERENA: Let's go and meet them. Come on everyone.

CHARLES: Give them the slow handclap.

SERENA: Come on.

BRIONY: No, I'll stay in. I just had…

CHARLES: A bidet. Yes, we know. Here, stick these somewhere.

(He thrusts them into BRIONY's hands and turns to go. SERENA and KEITH exit.)

Funny little fuckers when they're plucked. Look like skinned babies.

(We hear a car horn and see headlights. As he exits he starts the slow handclap.)

Halloooo! *(Singing.)* Oh why are we waiting? Why are we waiting?

BRIONY sinks into the chair and looks down at the plucked and headless birds as we hear the exchange of greetings outside. She bursts into tears. Blackout.

SCENE TWO

Two hours later, the six of them are seated on chairs or on the floor, having eaten their plates of cottage pie. Twenty or so shopping bags stand on the worktop. Bottles of wine are open, candles lit, and the atmosphere is much more relaxed. ROSS and ROSY are holding hands and ROSS is in full flight...

ROSS: Supposedly she'd looked after kids before. She had all the accreditation, the papers. I mean, the agencies vet these girls really thoroughly, because obviously there are thousands of young things out there, especially in Eastern Europe, who reckon they're onto something. You know? They come over here from some Balkan backwater and live in a million pound house for free. They walk a pair of nicely-behaved kids to school and back and that's their work done for the day. If they're really lucky they'll land a couple of tortured liberals like us who feel so guilty about the money we've made that we can't bring ourselves to ask them to iron the odd shirt, let alone clean around the rim of the lavatory, so they sit around all day in their big houses, painting their nails and scoffing their employers' organic chocolates...

ROSY: Yours maybe. I don't touch the stuff.

ROSS: Before vomiting them back up into the loo.

ROSY: Oh, Ross.

ROSS: How else would they fit into those terrible, too-tight trousers?

ROSY: Too tight, and bright white.

ROSS: Flared. With rhinestones across the buttocks.

ROSY: We'd always gone for Germans and Italians before, as you know. Now with those girls you know where you stand. They're from good families. They're sensible. And they might just expose your children to a different language that might be of some use to them one day.

ROSS: As opposed to Serbo-Croat.

ROSY: Which always sounds like a bad case of laryngitis.

ROSS: But the problem with Europeans – Western ones – is that they're actually…

BRIONY: Afraid of work?

ROSS: Well, yes, but so are the ones from Eastern Europe. They're all lazy sods. They're only eighteen, some of them. We're resigned to the laziness bit. No, it's gratitude that's missing. I mean, having some stranger in your house, blocking up the shower, the telephone line…

ROSY: Putting things back in the wrong place.

ROSS: Books.

ROSY: Clothes, cutlery.

ROSS: Just generally getting in your way.

ROSY: It's a nightmare.

ROSS: But at least the ones from the East are suitably grateful to be lifted out of poverty for a while. Yelena was no exception. And anyway, at the age of nearly forty I could do without the temptation of the organic chocolates.

ROSY: Which is all by way of saying that, too-tight trousers aside, Yelena seemed too good to be true.

ROSS: 'Seemed' being the operative word. Rosy?

ROSY: I don't know whether any of you remember our first au pair?

ROSS: Carlotta.

ROSY: From Naples.

CHARLES: Lovely girl.

SERENA: Shame about the face.

ROSY: Exactly. But she was very good with Rollo when Hebe came along.

ROSS: And then we had Gudrun. The Swede.

KEITH: Oh, he was great.

BRIONY: Keith, don't. It wasn't her fault.

KEITH: The weightlifting was.

ROSS: Not the terrible skin and the flame-red hair.

ROSY: But she was very good with the kids.

ROSS: Until we started thinking they might catch something.

ROSY: And that's when good old Heidi came to us.

ROSS: Come back Heidi, all is forgiven.

ROSY: All in all, we were pretty lucky, when you hear what other people go through.

ROSS: Until Yelena.

ROSY: Ross?

ROSS: Yelena was our first good-looking au pair.

ROSY: Not by accident.

ROSS: Rosy simply couldn't trust me alone in the house with anyone prettier than my own backside.

ROSY: Darling, your backside is beautiful.

ROSS: I wouldn't know.

ROSY: I would trust him to the end of the earth and he knows it. It's the girls I don't trust. They very often make a play for the man of the household.

ROSS: Sometimes with disastrous effect.

ROSY: A friend of my sister in Wimbledon just got divorced. Husband ran off with the au pair.

ROSS: There were problems in the marriage though.

ROSY: True.

ROSS: But even with a totally happy set-up, these girls can come in and stir up all sorts of trouble. Make up stuff. Lie and extort.

ROSY: Which is why we always said we'd go for…you know…

SERENA: Ugs.

CHARLES: Mingers.

KEITH: Munters.

BRIONY: Keith.

ROSY: Girls with unfortunate looks. And that way we'd simply avoid any of that nonsense. Young gold-diggers making up stories. Because handsome men don't go for ugly girls and everyone knows that.

ROSS: It was also for the kids. There's so much terrible lookism in the world and we didn't like the idea of having women in our house who were always gazing in the mirror – of exposing our own children to that.

ROSY: Yelena's photograph certainly didn't do her justice, did it?

ROSS: It must have been taken months before she arrived.

ROSY: Months before the dieting began.

ROSS: Imagine our faces when she turned up at Heathrow.

ROSY: We knew it wouldn't last.

ROSS: She was good with the kids.

ROSY: Terrific. Hebe knows all about French nails at the age of three.

ROSS: She liked them, though.

ROSY: Of course she did.

ROSS: And they liked her.

ROSY: We all liked her. She was funny.

ROSS: A little bit crazy, in that Eastern European way.

ROSY: Little did we know.

ROSS: Go on.

ROSY: No, you tell.

ROSS: Well, she's been with us…six months?

ROSY: Six and a half.

ROSS: And the kids really like her, and she's even starting to do a bit more around the house – like flushing after she's vomited – no, but you know, a bit of hoovering, a bit of cooking. And as I say, she's grateful. Polite and grateful. And it's actually okay having her around the place.

ROSY: In spite of the trousers.

ROSS: So I offer to give her another twenty quid a week – in recognition of all this.

ROSY: And she's overjoyed.

ROSS: She says she'll send it back to her village every week.

ROSY: Twenty quid is obviously a lot of money to her.

ROSS: She's very, very grateful. Which is nice. It'll mean that her old grandfather might just be able to have some operation he's been needing.

ROSY: And then?

ROSS: Then I get that virus. Remember? Last month. I was in bed for a fortnight.

ROSY: Poor darling.

ROSS: Sick as a dog. Thought I was dying.

ROSY: It was actually pretty serious. And I think Yelena knew that.

ROSS: She did. She knew I was vulnerable.

ROSY: She came into our bedroom one afternoon and asked him if he wanted any extra jobs to be done.

BRIONY: No.

CHARLES: Christ.

ROSS: I know.

KEITH: What sort of jobs?

BRIONY: Keith.

SERENA: Three guesses.

KEITH: Thank you. I mean, did she spell it out? Did she say what sort of jobs?

ROSS: She didn't have to.

ROSY: It was implicit.

CHARLES: Was she any good?

SERENA: Chas.

BRIONY: What did you do?

ROSY: He thanked her for the offer but let her know it was
totally unnecessary. He was utterly unequivocal, weren't
you?

ROSS: Utterly.

ROSY: Cut to:

ROSS: Last night, in our kitchen. I'm woken by the sound of
sobbing. I wander downstairs and find Yelena sitting on the
floor.

ROSY: Not wearing very much.

ROSS: She's got a T-shirt on.

CHARLES: Knickers?

ROSY: Technically, yes.

ROSS: She's very upset about something. So I sit down and
put an arm around her. Who wouldn't? Turns out her
grandad's operation didn't go according to plan – a cancer
thing – and he's heard of some genius doctor in London
who's got all the answers and she's suddenly asking me
to lend her three grand. Or give it to her, really. I mean,
how's she going to pay it back?

CHARLES: Hundred and fifty extra little jobs?

ROSS: So I have to be tough with her. I say 'Listen Yelena, it's
not going to happen. I'm sorry. Go back to bed.'

SERENA: And does she?

ROSY: Not before she takes her T-shirt off. That's when I walk
in.

CHARLES: Fuck.

ROSS: I'm like 'Whoa, girl'. You know? Bosoms out.

ROSY: If you can call them that.

ROSS: Nought to sixty in one second. Fortunately I am
married to an extremely bright, unthreatened woman who
sees immediately the truth of the situation. She says 'Put

your shirt back on, Yelena. He's not interested. We're going back to bed.'

KEITH: Wow.

CHARLES: Well done.

ROSS: Cut to:

ROSY: Our bedroom, half an hour later. Yelena has slipped a note under our bedroom door – addressed to Ross – pointing out that unless she gets the money today she will tell me everything.

ROSS: Which means, of course, nothing.

ROSY: So we both go up to her room in the attic.

ROSS: And Rosy says:

ROSY: 'Go ahead, Yelena. Kiss and tell. We're all ears.'

ROSS: It's kind of scary, when you realise how little you've known someone that's actually been living under your roof.

ROSY: The delusions. She's certainly got an imagination. I'll give her that.

ROSS: Oh, apparently in that fortnight I'd been ill we'd had some sort of Olympian sex fest.

ROSY: Up and down the stairs, on the kitchen table.

ROSS: In our marital bed.

ROSY: Don't. That really got me cross. As she knew it would.

ROSS: We'd done it literally all over the house.

KEITH: What, everywhere?

ROSS: All over the house.

KEITH: Not in the…the kids' rooms?

BRIONY: Keith.

KEITH: What?

ROSY: No, fortunately there was some scrap of decency in the woman that kept her lurid imaginings away from the sanctity of the third floor.

BRIONY: Thank God.

ROSY: I know.

BRIONY: But still.

ROSY: I know.

BRIONY: The little viper. What a nerve. After all you'd done for her, to blackmail you like that. Did you call the police?

ROSY: Of course not, because everyone knew it was complete and utter fabrication. We actually laughed. Didn't we?

ROSS: Yes.

ROSY: In her face.

ROSS: Which didn't go down that well.

ROSY: She obviously realised there wasn't the tiniest chink in our armour. We stood there, holding hands, and laughing at what a preposterous suggestion it was.

ROSS: She was gone within twenty minutes.

ROSY: I actually gave her two hundred quid.

ROSS: You felt sorry for her.

ROSY: We both did.

ROSS: Desperate.

ROSY: Desperate and deranged. We still haven't really explained it properly to Rollo and Hebe. And that, finally, ladies and gentlemen, is why we were uncharacteristically late. I thought we'd be all right but we had to go via Bristol to drop the kids off with friends.

ROSS: And then we got snarled up in traffic on the M49.

BRIONY: God.

KEITH: What a story.

ROSY: A minor hiccup.

ROSS: We rang the agency today and there's a new girl arriving on Tuesday.

ROSY: Dutch.

ROSS: Face like the back end of a barge.

ROSY: And the size of a small dyke, by the look of it.

CHARLES: Well, if she starts leaking, don't go sticking your finger in!

BRIONY: Amazing. I really don't know how you do it.

ROSY: It's easy. I have complete faith in my husband.

BRIONY: Both of you. You just deal with life so well.

ROSS: These things are sent to try us.

KEITH: I want to know when you found time to make the cottage pie.

ROSY: Shepherd's.

KEITH: Shepherd's then.

ROSY: Major confession I'm afraid. I made a double batch a couple of weeks ago and stuck it in the freezer.

KEITH: It was delicious.

BRIONY: Yes, it really was.

ROSY: Good.

ROSS: Briony's right. You are amazing. Come here.

He kisses her.

BRIONY: Aw.

CHARLES: What's the difference anyway?

ROSS: Between what?

BRIONY: Really, I don't know how you do it.

CHARLES: Shepherd's and cottage. I've never known.

ROSY: It's dead easy.

BRIONY: I don't just mean…

ROSS: Shepherd's pie is made with minced lamb. Cottage pie is made with minced Tory MPs. They free-range all over Clapham Common.

CHARLES: MPs?

SERENA: Oh they all need a good mincing.

ROSY: I don't think cottaging is restricted to Tories.

CHARLES: I'm lost.

BRIONY: So am I.

ROSS: It's a gay thing.

CHARLES: Is it?

ROSS: I'm afraid so.

ROSY: Actually it's beef.

CHARLES: What is?

ROSY: Cottage pie. It's beef.

CHARLES: Whatever floats your boat. We had a few gays in the army. They were actually quite decent fellows.

KEITH: Why cottage though?

CHARLES: What?

SERENA: Something to do with lavatories.

ROSS: Small buildings. Generally one storey.

KEITH: Yes, I know that but…

ROSY: And cottage has a much nicer ring to it than bungalow.

ROSS: Let's keep our rings out of it, shall we? *(ROSY groans.)* Sorry.

BRIONY: So why's it called cottage cheese?

ROSS: Shall we talk about something else?

KEITH: But really, I mean what's wrong with cowherd's?

SERENA: Sorry?

KEITH: Cowherd's pie.

CHARLES: Doesn't sound right.

KEITH: Well, no. We're not used to it, that's why.

SERENA: There's no such thing as a cowherd.

KEITH: Of course there is. Once on a hill stood a lonely…

ROSS: Goatherd?

KEITH: Oh yes.

BRIONY: I don't just mean the pie though, Rosy.

ROSY: Hmm?

BRIONY: You just…manage. You cope with things so well.

ROSY: Do we? Maybe. I don't know.

SERENA: Cowboy. Cowgirl.

BRIONY: You never let things faze you.

KEITH: Cowherd. Someone that herds cows.

SERENA: Well, you can stick herd after anything. Duckherd. Catherd.

ROSY: Anyway…

BRIONY: You're so on top of it all. This thing with the au pair. I'd have gone off the deep end.

ROSY: That wasn't an option.

SERENA: Moleherd. Tapirherd.

CHARLES: Moleherd!

BRIONY: You're just so good at life.

SERENA: Spirogyraherd.

KEITH: That's ridiculous.

BRIONY: How do you do it?

SERENA: Why?

ROSY: Inner-strength.

SERENA: Why is it any more ridiculous than cowherd?

ROSY: Ross and I both do yoga. If you don't control life, life turns round and starts controlling you.

BRIONY: But that means having confidence in yourself. You can't just decide to be confident.

ROSY: Of course you can.

SERENA: If I'm herding spirogyra, why can't I call myself a spirogyraherd?

KEITH: Because nobody herds spirogyra.

SERENA: How do you know what I do in my spare time?

ROSS: I think you should agree to disagree.

BRIONY: You can't just change who you are.

SERENA: We're having fun, aren't we, Keith?

KEITH: I suppose so.

SERENA: We're inventing words.

BRIONY: Well, I can't.

SERENA: Cowherd, for example.

KEITH: No, I'm sorry, you're wrong. There are definitely people out there who herd cows. They are called cowherds, and it is therefore not ridiculous to suggest that an alternative name for cottage pie might be cowherd's pie. But there is no one who herds moles or spirogyra.

SERENA: How do you know?

KEITH: Because they're single-celled organisms!

BRIONY: Keith.

KEITH: No, I'm sorry, but I won't be talked down to like this.

ROSS: I think you should calm down.

SERENA: I'm not talking down to you.

KEITH: Yes you are.

ROSS: She's not.

KEITH: She is. She always does. She thinks she's so much…

BRIONY: Keith!

SERENA: What?

ROSY: We really don't need to be doing this.

ROSS: No, we don't.

SERENA: What do I think I am?

ROSY: Who'd like some pudding? Plum crumble and cream.

SERENA: What do I think I am? Go on.

BRIONY: It doesn't matter. Leave it. Keith. Go outside and cool off.

KEITH: I'm fine.

BRIONY: You're not. You're drunk. Go outside. *(KEITH hesitates.)* Keith.

KEITH: I'm not a child.

BRIONY: Well, stop behaving like one then.

KEITH: I'm going to go and read.

KEITH goes to the bedroom.

BRIONY: Sorry. We're both quite stressed at the moment.

ROSS: We know. That's why we arranged this weekend.

ROSY: It's going to do us all a power of good to be away from the pressure of work – and kids.

BRIONY: Kids, yes. Our lives are so dominated by them. I don't know how the rest of you manage.

CHARLES: The more you have, the easier it gets.

SERENA: That's true.

BRIONY: I forget how many you have.

CHARLES: So do I. How many do we have?

SERENA: Silly arse. Four or five.

ROSY: You're not sticking on one, are you?

BRIONY: Maybe. I just think…

ROSY: It'll be very hard on Finn. You think you're doing him a favour…

BRIONY: No, I…

ROSY: But it'll create a lot of trouble for him in later life.

ROSS: And now too. They have to learn to share, Briony. And if they can share their parents, they can share anything.

ROSY: We find that two is the perfect number. Everything's nicely balanced. And it does take the pressure off us, doesn't it?

ROSS: Yes.

ROSY: Gives us some downtime.

SERENA: Don't listen to them. There's no secret bloody formula. You could have another kid and he might turn out to be a right little shit...

ROSY: No, not if you...

SERENA: Or you could stick on one, and he could turn out perfectly fine. It's nothing to do with you though, that's the point.

ROSS: You honestly can't stick on one. It's so selfish.

CHARLES: I'm an only child, and look at me! *(Pause.)* Well, I did have five siblings, but I shot them all.

ROSY: I really am an only child, and I don't recommend it.

ROSS: Maybe you should use this weekend to...you know...

ROSY: Ross!

CHARLES: I don't think she needs any prompting, do you?

BRIONY: What?

CHARLES: You don't need us telling you what to do. We're all too bloody interfering these days. Pills for this, advice for that. Nature takes care of it. We didn't do a bloody thing, did we? Four little buggers just popped out.

SERENA: Five.

CHARLES: Five. She knew she was ready, every time, like a randy sow.

SERENA: Ooh Charlie.

CHARLIE: She came and found me, wherever I was, and she said 'Now, Chas. Do it to me now', which I thought was bloody marvellous, and so we did it, in a cupboard, a field, wherever. You let nature dictate.

SERENA: Emphasis on the dic.

ROSS: I just meant you should talk to Keith about it.

ROSY: Plum crumble anyone?

CHARLIE: Love some.

ROSY gets up and dishes out the pudding.

ROSS: Anyway, we're not interfering. We're just saying that maybe Keith is…maybe you're both stressed because…

BRIONY: Because we need another baby?

ROSS: And because in trying…well, you won't hit the jackpot every time.

CHARLIE: We bloody did!

BRIONY: What are you saying, Ross?

CHARLES: I tell you, the filly doesn't need any prompting!

ROSY: He's saying you can have a lot of fun. It can be very anxiety-provoking, the whole idea of…but at some point you've got to…

ROSS: Get back on the horse.

ROSY: Or let him get back on.

SERENA: Feet in the stirrups. Crop in hand.

CHARLES: There won't be a problem after tomorrow. I'm taking the man out.

BRIONY: Problem?

ROSS: We're not saying there's a problem.

ROSY hands CHARLES his pudding.

ROSY: Crumble? Briony?

BRIONY: What?

ROSY: Plum crumble.

SERENA: His plums aren't crumbling. He just needs an hour with Charles.

BRIONY: Has Keith been talking to you about our sex life?

ROSS: No.

ROSY: Serena? Pudding?

SERENA: Fuck me, definitely. Bags of cream.

BRIONY: He has.

ROSY: You'll have some, won't you, Ross?

ROSS: Yes please.

BRIONY: Keith!

ROSS: He hasn't. I swear.

BRIONY gets up and walks over to the bedroom door.

BRIONY: I don't believe you.

ROSY: Have some crumble, Briony.

BRIONY: I don't want any bloody crumble. I'm fat enough as it is. Keith!

KEITH: *(Off.)* What?

BRIONY: I want you out here now.

KEITH: *(Off.)* I'm reading.

BRIONY: Now, Keith. Don't make me shout at you.

ROSS: Honestly, Briony.

BRIONY: Five seconds.

ROSS: He didn't say a thing…

BRIONY: One. I'm counting.

SERENA: Aren't you having any?

BRIONY: Two.

ROSY: I don't eat puddings.

SERENA: Why? You're thin as a rake.

BRIONY: Three.

ROSY: Oh, it's not because of that.

ROSS: Briony.

ROSY: I'm actually highly allergic to sugar.

BRIONY: Four.

ROSY: I'd love to pig out on stuff like that, but it's too dangerous.

BRIONY: Five. *(Yelling.)* Keith Ragg, you come out…!

KEITH appears as she begins to shout.

Have you been talking to Ross about our sex life?

KEITH: No.

BRIONY: Do you promise?

KEITH: Yes.

BRIONY: On Finn's life?

SERENA: Oh come on.

BRIONY: Don't interfere please.

ROSY: Briony.

BRIONY: Do you, Keith?

ROSS: You shouldn't play around with this sort of thing.

KEITH: He's right.

BRIONY: You're the one who's playing around. Our sex life is private.

KEITH: I know.

BRIONY: Well, why have you been talking about it then?

KEITH: I haven't.

BRIONY: Swear then. On Finn's life.

KEITH: No, I won't.

BRIONY: Then you're lying.

KEITH: Just because I won't swear on his life, it doesn't mean I'm lying. It just means I'm not comfortable swearing on his life. He's three years old for fuck's sake.

44

BRIONY: Don't swear at me, Keith Ragg.

KEITH: Stop doing that.

BRIONY: What?

KEITH: Using my surname.

BRIONY: I can do what I like, Keith Ragg. Promise me on Finn's life.

KEITH: No, Briony.

BRIONY: Why? If you're telling the truth, it won't matter.

KEITH: Yes it will.

BRIONY: Why?

KEITH: Because I love him. I love him much more than you do.

(BRIONY stands up.)

I didn't…

BRIONY: Excuse me.

She runs into the bedroom and slams the door. We hear her weeping.

KEITH: Shit.

ROSY: Plum crumble?

KEITH: What? Er…yes. Please.

ROSS: Sorry.

KEITH: It's all right. She's suffering from depression, and she didn't bring her medication. She thinks she's all right without it, but she isn't.

CHARLES: P'raps you should both come out with me tomorrow.

SERENA: Charles. Shut it.

CHARLES: I've seen it work. The best medication is to…

SERENA: Back in your box. Or I'll take your batteries out.

CHARLES: Right-oh.

ROSY: She'll probably feel better after a good night's sleep.

She hands KEITH his pudding.

KEITH: She's so scared of failing. She knows it's good for her to be away from Finn, but she feels guilty. She feels bad when she's with him, and even worse when they're apart.

ROSY: It's important to let go.

ROSS: Crucial.

KEITH: Are you sure you can't get a signal?

ROSS: Positive.

KEITH: Maybe I should drive to a phone-box.

ROSY: You've had too much to drink. We all have.

ROSS: Anyway, I told you, it's sorted. It's all arranged with the owner. He's the local farmer. Your parents have got his number, haven't they?

KEITH: Yes.

ROSS: I e-mailed it to everyone. In case mobiles didn't work. That's what failsafe means.

KEITH: Could I try your phone? Just to see.

ROSS: It's a dead zone. Trust me. He'll drive up here if there's any urgent message. He's reliable. Rosy spoke to him on the phone.

ROSY: Not the friendliest individual.

ROSS: He's a busy man.

KEITH: Exactly. He'll be out all day, herding cows.

ROSS: Then his wife will take the message.

ROSY: He's a widower actually.

ROSS: All right, his ansaphone then.

ROSY: He has a disabled son.

ROSS: Oh yes, I forgot. His son'll take the message.

KEITH: If he can.

ROSS: I'm sure he can answer a phone.

KEITH: Depends though, doesn't it? Depends on his disability.

ROSY: Oh Keith.

KEITH: I'm just saying. He might not be able to.

ROSS: Listen, when we told him we were held up in traffic the man took the time to come up here and unlock the place. He's efficient. Stop fretting. We're all in the same boat, Keith. All our kids are fine.

ROSY: Go in there and make it up to her. Say you're sorry. Reassure her.

KEITH: I might start off with a quick neck rub. She likes that.

(Headlights are seen outside, and we hear brakes screech. ROSS goes to look.)

Oh no.

ROSY: Who the hell is that?

KEITH: It's the farmer. Fuck, I bet it's Finn. A message about Finn. Please don't let it be Finn.

ROSS: Doubt it's the farmer.

KEITH: Why?

ROSS: It's an open-top sports car. If it is him, he's got fabulous legs.

CHARLES: Tabby!

SERENA: Shit.

ROSY: Tabby? Who's Tabby?

CHARLES: Her niece. Right little minx.

SERENA: She's going through a terrible time.

ROSS: How did she know how to get here?

SERENA: We gave her the address. She split up with her boyfriend yesterday.

CHARLES: It's not the way I thought it would end. He's eighty-two, the dirty old sod. Still, good on him.

ROSY: Well, she can't stay. All the rooms are full. She'll have to drive to…where is it? Aberga…thingy.

47

CHARLES: She can kip with us. I'll sleep in the car.

ROSS: There's a perfectly good sofa.

ROSY: Ross!

The door opens and TABBY comes in. She's dead on her feet. Her clothes are falling off, she has a bruise above her eye, and her make-up is badly smeared.

SERENA: Tab.

CHARLES: Christ. You look fucking awful.

She dumps her bag, takes a handful of crumble and stuffs it in her mouth. She begins to laugh hysterically, throws her arms around the horrified ROSY and then teeters over to the sofa and collapses. CHARLES laughs.

ROSY: Ross?

Blackout.

SCENE THREE

The next day, 12 noon. The sofa has been turned into a bed, and TABBY's stuff is all over it. ROSS is alone in the house, preparing lunch. A counter obscures him from the waist down – a fact that will be of significance later. He listens to Radio 4 while he cuts vegetables. A knock at the door. It's the farmer, MORGAN.

ROSS: Mr. Morgan? Huw, isn't it? How's it going?

MORGAN: I didn't know if there was anyone here. I saw five or six figures way up in the top field, heading diagonally over. Your lot, are they?

ROSS: Yes, my wife loves her walks. She frogmarched them out of here straight after breakfast.

MORGAN: Tell them to stick to the path in future, will you please? Those fields are valuable pasture for my livestock.

ROSS: Sorry.

MORGAN: That's what the paths are for.

ROSS: Yes. I'm sorry.

MORGAN: The agency assures me it states quite explicitly on the what-do-you-call-it…computer…

ROSS: Website?

MORGAN: It states unambiguously that children and pets are not welcome and that the adjacent farmland must be treated with respect.

ROSS: Understood.

MORGAN: Responsible adults only. This is working land. Not a playground.

ROSS: Absolutely. Anyway, what can I do for you?

MORGAN: I had a telephone call this morning. In fact my son took it as I was out milking. It had to wait till I came back on account of my son's physical handicap.

ROSS: Of course.

MORGAN: He's confined to a wheelchair, see. So he couldn't come and find me. And I don't hold with mobile telephones.

ROSS: What was the message?

MORGAN: A lady by the name of Ragg.

ROSS: Oh, right.

MORGAN: The mother of one of your party.

ROSS: That's it.

MORGAN: Pleasant sounding person. Very polite. I believe her husband served in the police force.

ROSS: What was the message?

MORGAN: We had a very nice chat. She inquired about my circumstances, but in a very respectful way.

ROSS: Right.

MORGAN: You don't always get that.

ROSS: No.

MORGAN: I told her about my son. She was terribly sympathetic. I believe her son was quite sickly when he was young.

ROSS: Keith? Was he?

MORGAN: I believe so. Bringing up a sick child is not easy, especially when you're trying to run a farm.

ROSS: Quite.

MORGAN: Especially in the last few years. BSE. Foot and mouth. EU regulations.

ROSS: Right.

MORGAN: Especially when you're a widower.

ROSS: Anyway. Oh, I'm so sorry. Was it a long…?

MORGAN: Ten years ago next week. My boy was only six. We wouldn't have made it through without the constant love of him who suffered most. Do you have Jesus Christ in your heart?

ROSS: Oh God. Oh, God. Oh, yes.

MORGAN: Good. What church do you attend?

ROSS: The local one.

MORGAN: Which is that?

ROSS: Do you know Clapham very well?

MORGAN: No.

ROSS: Well, it's next to a big wine bar at the top end of…

MORGAN: High church or low?

ROSS: Actually I think the steeple was damaged by a…

MORGAN: What denomination?

ROSS: Oh, Christian. Definitely Christian.

MORGAN: There are many kinds of Christians. Serious and fair-weather.

ROSS: Right. Listen, about the message…

MORGAN: Trendy Christians. They've all got a bit of the devil in them.

ROSS: Oh, well.

MORGAN: If you don't know what denomination you are, I'd suggest you're fair-weather.

ROSS: On the contrary, I'm terribly serious about Christianity. In fact, that is why we're here. It's a retreat. There's no space in the city for proper prayer – you know, a good five hour session. So we came here. For some silence – shut up! *(Turns off the radio.)* God! Bloody radio. I'm preparing a simple, homely roast dinner with all the trimmings, which we shall eat today before fasting all day tomorrow, while the others are out communing with Nature, at one with God's creation, sticking as far as possible to the path – of righteousness.

MORGAN: Do I detect a mocking tone?

ROSS: I've never been more serious in my entire life. Now, in God's name I beg you: the message?

MORGAN: I don't think it's that urgent.

ROSS: Evidently.

MORGAN: The lady said her grandson...

ROSS: Finn...

MORGAN: That's it. He's been taken into hospital.

ROSS: What?

MORGAN: They all went in the ambulance.

ROSS: What's wrong with him?

MORGAN: He was screaming with pain.

ROSS: Why?

MORGAN: They tried to sedate him. But apparently he screamed even more when he saw the hypodermic syringe.

ROSS: Mr. Morgan.

MORGAN: Yes?

ROSS: What's the matter with him?

MORGAN: He's broken a toe.

ROSS: A toe?

MORGAN: Kicked the bedroom door. Temper tantrum.
They've put his foot in plaster and he's back at home now.

ROSS: Oh.

MORGAN: If I'd kicked my bedroom door when I was his age
I'd have been caned.

ROSS: Did she say anything else?

MORGAN: She said it was all fine. And the child's parents
should on no account curtail their holiday. She didn't
mention anything about a retreat.

ROSS: It's Keith's little secret from his old mother.

MORGAN: Secret?

ROSS: She's a devout atheist. Finding Jesus was Keith's greatest
rebellion.

MORGAN: She sounded so nice.

ROSS: Wolf in sheep's clothing. Anyway, thank you, Huw.
Really good of you to bring the message up.

*TABBY enters, out of breath, looking the very opposite of a young
Christian.*

TABBY: Fuck me.

MORGAN: Who is this?

ROSS: No idea. Who are you?

TABBY: Very funny. I'm fucked. This fresh air's killing me. Is
lunch ready yet? Cos I'm starving. Where's the booze?

MORGAN: Is she a member of your party?

TABBY: Party? If this is a party, bruv, it's the driest I ever been
at. The gear is like totally scarce.

ROSS: This is Tabby. We are hoping to bring her to the light.
Tabby is a troubled soul but not beyond hope. Indeed she
helps us all to give thanks for what we have, compared
to what she has, which is nothing, apart from a flat on the
King's Road and a convertible Saab, but a little like our
Saviour, she is doing her level best to rid herself of all her
worldly possessions.

TABBY: Fuck off.

TABBY has poured herself a glass of wine and got back into bed.

MORGAN: May I ask how old you are?

TABBY: You can ask.

ROSS: Seventeen.

MORGAN: Only a year older than my son. God help you. I must get back to him. His disability prevents him from doing even the simplest task. You'll pass the message on?

ROSS: Of course.

MORGAN: Nothing to worry about, she said. Anyway, enjoy your time here.

ROSS: Goodbye. And thanks again.

TABBY: Oh fuck. I need a piss.

She gets out of bed and goes off into one of the bedrooms.

MORGAN: If the wind blows in the wrong direction tonight, you'll none of you sleep a wink. There's a rave in the next valley. I'd keep her locked up if I were you. They come from miles around, with their illegal substances. On such occasions as these I give thanks for my son's disability.

He goes. ROSS pours himself a glass of wine. Finds his mobile and makes a call.

ROSS: Hello, Ross here. Message for Granny and Grandpa Ragg. Just heard about poor old Finn. Dear oh dear. Well, that'll teach him to have tantrums, won't it? But glad he's okay and I'm sure you're right – he'll survive without mum and dad till Monday. All the best. Bye.

He drinks some wine. TABBY re-enters.

TABBY: Has he gone?

ROSS: Looks like it.

TABBY: What a fucking moron. What was all that Christian bollocks?

ROSS: Where's Rosy?

TABBY: She was getting on my tits, so I came back. I'm boiling, man. My body ain't used to all this exercise. I'm crippled.

ROSS: She believes in building up an appetite.

TABBY: That's why God gave us spliff. Bet Rosy don't let you have no spliff.

ROSS: Why do you say that?

TABBY: She got you well trained.

ROSS: I don't know what you mean.

TABBY: Cooking in your apron. Batty boy don't get no fun.

ROSS: Oh I see, not content with gate-crashing this weekend, you think it's acceptable to start laying into your hosts.

TABBY: Bet you ain't never even tried it.

ROSS: What? Dope?

TABBY: Bet she ain't neither. Bet you fink half a bottle of this shit is real dangerous livin'.

ROSS: You're very annoying, aren't you?

TABBY: I can read you so clear, Mister Square-boy. Fuck, I'm so hot. Fucking fresh air, man.

ROSS: Perhaps you're about to die. Oh well, never mind.

TABBY: You fink you're so clever, don't you, square-boy?

ROSS: Oh dear. Can't you put your i-Pod on and listen to some lovely uplifting gangsta-rap hip-hop garage?

TABBY: So funny and so clever. I'd give a lot of bills to see you totally out of your box.

ROSS: How sweet of you. I'm actually extremely happy in my box, and now, if you don't mind, I'm going to get back to the lunch preparations.

TABBY: OK, batty boy.

ROSS: I fail to see how my enjoyment of the culinary arts and general willingness to do my share of domestic chores could possibly have a bearing on sexual preference. I'm presuming that 'batty boy' is your Naffro-Caribbean way of saying 'botty boy' and therefore an attempted slur on my heterosexual credentials, but in fact I have a number of very good friends who are homosexual, so it's no particular insult to me to be considered one of their number.

TABBY: Twat.

He puts the radio back on and carries on with his preparations. He turns away to wash something in the sink. TABBY strips to her panties. ROSS turns back and picks up a chopping knife. ROSS looks up and, practically jumping out of his skin, drops the knife, which lands – out of view – in his foot.

ROSS: Fuck! Shit!

TABBY laughs, and gets back into bed.

Jesus. Aaaargh!

TABBY: Maybe you ain't no batty boy after all.

ROSS: No, I've… Jesus!

(He comes round from behind the counter and we see that the knife is stuck straight down into his foot. There is blood.)

Look. Look!

TABBY: Sick.

ROSS: Do something, will you?

TABBY: Like what?

ROSS: How should I know?

TABBY: You don't want to pull it out, bro.

ROSS: Why?

TABBY: It'll go all Reservoir Dogs. The blade is acting like a cork. Looks cool, though, fam.

ROSS: Fuck! Why did you…? What were you doing, stripping off like that?

TABBY: I told you, I was hot. Has square-boy never seen naked totty before?

ROSS: Stop calling me square-boy! Aaah! *(He sits on the sofa bed.)* Help me.

TABBY: I ain't touching it.

ROSS: Please.

TABBY: Got to be careful with blood. Could be dirty.

ROSY is heard outside.

ROSY: *(Off.)* Tabby!

ROSS: Oh Jesus, no. Put some clothes on, will you?

TABBY: Why?

ROSS: Just do it!

TABBY: Don't she trust you or somefing?

ROSS: Now!

TABBY: Lickle Tabby just helping to get you out of your box, city-boy. Relax. Bit of jealousy is good for a 'ealthy marriage.

ROSS: Please!

TABBY: Don't tell me square-boy has been playing away from home?

ROSS: Fucking idiot.

ROSY: *(Off.)* Tabby!

ROSS: Put your fucking clothes on.

TABBY: Make me, victim of knife-crime.

ROSS: Fucking nutter.

ROSY enters, followed by KEITH, BRIONY, SERENA & CHARLES.

ROSY: Ross, has that bloody girl come…?

TABBY: Think yourself lucky you only got it in the foot, you fucker. You jump these baby bones again, you get it in the face. You hear me, paedy-boy? Don't you fucking mess with me!

Blackout.

Act Two

SCENE ONE

The early hours. Things are quiet – ish. When the wind gusts we hear music from the next valley. TABBY's bed appears to contain a sleeping figure. ROSY emerges from her bedroom. She drinks some water and then goes towards the sofa bed. She is about to pull back the sheet when, out of the shadows, a voice speaks:

BRIONY: Hello.

ROSY: Bloody hell.

BRIONY: Sorry. Trouble sleeping?

ROSY: Yes.

BRIONY: The music?

ROSY: Ross's foot. He keeps groaning and twitching in his sleep.

(She goes to the sink and pours herself a glass of water.)

Good excuse to drink some water. I'm very big on rehydration.

BRIONY: I never bother.

ROSY: Oh you must.

BRIONY: I hate the taste.

ROSY: There is no taste.

BRIONY: The lack of taste then.

ROSY: Nonsense. Here. *(Hands her a glass.)* Go on. Drink it all down. It's very important. What's Keith like?

BRIONY: He hates it too.

ROSY: No, I mean in bed…

(BRIONY laughs and eventually ROSY does too.)

I mean, is he a groaner? Oh dear. You know what I mean.

BRIONY: Sleeps like a baby. It's all the grappling beforehand that's the trouble. He's all over me – like German measles. Funny expression, 'sleeps like a baby'. I mean, when Finn finally does go down he's fine, but it's never for long. He soon wakes up and wants to get at me, suck on me, like a leech. Keith's the same.

ROSY: *(Laughing.)* Yuck.

BRIONY: What?

ROSY: I thought you meant…oh, you did. Oh, that's disgusting.

BRIONY: He loves it.

ROSY: I feel sick.

BRIONY: I don't let him do it very often. I need it for Finn.

ROSY: But I don't understand. You can't still be…

BRIONY: I thought you knew. I've wanted to stop for ages, but Finn still really wants it. You don't approve.

ROSY: Each to her own, Briony but no, it's pretty gross. He's a big boy now.

BRIONY: So is Finn.

ROSY: I meant Finn. I stopped at six months. We both knew, baby and I, both times. We were ready to move on to the next stage. If you're not firm, then how will they ever learn? You have to be firm.

BRIONY: I used to be wonderfully firm.

ROSY: Well, no wonder. You're not giving yourself a chance. And I don't know what you're doing allowing Keith to…

BRIONY: I don't.

ROSY: Well, you have done, evidently.

BRIONY: Very occasionally. Anyway, everyone does it.

ROSY: Not everyone.

BRIONY: Everyone tries it though.

ROSY: No.

BRIONY: Didn't Ross?

ROSY: Ross is very grown up. Why would he want breast-milk? He's a PR exec.

BRIONY: It's only milk. It's natural.

ROSY: Not when you're forty. When you're forty, it's obscene.

BRIONY: Any more obscene than drinking it from the udders of a farmyard animal?

ROSY: Perhaps you've never heard of pasteurisation. Anyway we only drink organic. *(She moves away then turns back.)* I don't like to interfere, Briony, but it does seem to me that you need to set clearer guidelines, for everyone's happiness. We all need boundaries. Or we turn out like her. Flashing ourselves at married men and making them skewer their feet to the floor. It's time to start weaning. Goodnight.

BRIONY: I'm glad Ross's foot's all right.

ROSY: Thank God for Dr. Serena. If only she had something in her bag for this one. They should book her into rehab.

BRIONY: You think that's what it was then?

ROSY: What?

BRIONY: With Ross. You think it was just her causing trouble?

ROSY: She's a drug addict. Listen, a lot of women find my husband attractive – witness the mad Balkan – but he would never, ever do anything to jeopardise what we have. He is devoted to me. Funny, when they're asleep, you can forgive them anything. There's probably quite a nice girl somewhere inside, beneath all that shit.

BRIONY: She must be sweltering under there.

ROSY: Basically a sweet kid, who's crying out for help.

BRIONY: Oh.

ROSY: What?

BRIONY: She's not sweltering. She's not here.

ROSY strides across and pulls back the covers.

ROSY: Lying little bitch. I don't believe it. Ross! She's gone to the bloody rave. Ross!

(ROSY now strides back to the bedroom and opens the door.)

Ross. Come out here. *(To BRIONY.)* She swore an oath. I suppose an oath means nothing to a girl like that. Christ, I could throttle her.

BRIONY: She's not your responsibility, Rosy.

ROSY: Whose is she then? Who organised this weekend?

BRIONY: She's Charles and Serena's.

ROSY: Don't be ridiculous. They can't control her.

ROSS enters, groggily. He limps, one foot bandaged. ROSY looks out the window.

ROSS: What's going on?

ROSY: She's gone. She's not here.

ROSS: Good.

ROSY: Her car's still here. She's gone to the rave.

ROSS: So?

ROSY: She's gone out looking for trouble.

ROSS: Well, I hope she finds it.

ROSY: Someone needs to take her in hand.

ROSS: I've got enough on my plate. Anyway, she's old enough to look after herself.

ROSY: She's only seventeen. Do you know what goes on at raves? We're not just talking dope. We're talking Class As. Ecstasy. Amphetamines. Heroin, Ross. We're talking desperate dropouts from the slums of Swansea.

ROSS: She'll be fine.

ROSY: No, she won't. She's only turned out like this because no one could be bothered to give her any parameters. She needs disciplining.

ROSS: Well, what do you want to do?

ROSY: Someone has to go out and find her.

ROSS: Don't look at me. I can barely walk.

BRIONY: I think you should wake up Charles.

ROSS: He was totally hammered when they went to bed. They both were.

ROSY: Briony's right. Wake him up, Ross.

ROSS: What? Why me?

ROSY: Why not?

ROSS: He's SAS trained. He'll break my fucking neck.

ROSY: Tabby's their niece. He's got to go out there and bring her home. She's out of control. Go on, Ross. I'm not having that girl's blood on my hands. Wake them up and tell them.

ROSS: All right.

ROSY: A good loud knock. Nice and firm.

ROSS: I know how to knock.

ROSY: Please don't be like that.

ROSS: I'm not.

He raps loudly on CHARLES and SERENA's door. No answer. He raps again.

ROSY: Really hammer on it.

ROSS: I am hammering.

ROSS hammers again. No answer.

ROSY: You'll have to go in.

ROSS: No, Rosy.

ROSY: Oh for heaven's sake. What do you think he's going to do to you?

ROSS: He was paralytic. You don't just wake people up – especially trained killers.

BRIONY: You should never wake a sleepwalker. They can be very violent.

ROSY: I really never had you down for a wimp.

She pushes past him and opens the door.

BRIONY: Be careful.

(ROSY goes in. Silence.)

She's right. I mean, just think if it were one of yours out there on some remote hillside.

ROSS: My children will never be the kind of people who would do that sort of thing. Never. All right?

BRIONY: You hope.

ROSS: No, Briony. I know.

BRIONY: Lucky you then.

ROSS: Nothing to do with luck, Briony. It's parameters.

BRIONY: There's no hope for little Finn then. None at all.

BRIONY starts to weep.

ROSS: Oh God.

ROSY re-enters.

ROSY: They're not there either.

ROSS: What?

ROSY: I don't fucking believe it!

ROSS: Are you sure?

ROSY: It might be the largest bedroom, Ross, but it's still only eighteen by fifteen.

ROSS: Did you check the ensuite?

ROSY: Of course I did.

ROSS: Where are they then?

ROSY: They've obviously gone to the rave as well.

ROSS: Maybe they went to find Tabby and bring her back.

ROSY: They were rat-arsed. And they don't give a damn. They take cocaine, Ross. They've probably gone to…what do you call it? Score. As if it wasn't enough that their druggy niece turns up. Well, I'm not fucking having it. They're not going to ruin my weekend.

ROSS: What are you doing?

ROSY: I'm going to get her.

ROSS: No, you're not.

ROSY: I am.

ROSS: Not on your own.

ROSY: Fine. Briony, get your boots on.

ROSS: You don't know what's out there. These are dangerous people. There could be hundreds of them, off their heads on chemicals.

ROSY: Exactly.

ROSS: Keith can go with you.

BRIONY: Why? What's wrong with me?

ROSS: You're very volatile at the moment.

BRIONY: No I'm not.

ROSS: You are, Briony.

BRIONY: I'm not! I'm thirty-eight and I teach reception. I don't know what Keith's been saying, but I'm all right. I miss my son, and Tabby being out there makes me... so don't tell me I can't go out there. Because I'm a good mother. I might not be the best mother, but I'm all right.

ROSY: Of course you are.

BRIONY: I'm all right.

ROSY: Finn's fine. All our kids are fine. Aren't they, Ross?

ROSS: What?

ROSY: All our kids are fine.

ROSS: Yes. They're fine. Go on then. Go and get her, if you must.

(ROSY and BRIONY are by this time booted and coated.)

Can I suggest you take a torch? There's one in the car.

ROSY: I am not an idiot.

ROSS: No?

ROSY: What's that supposed to mean?

ROSS: You're behaving like one.

ROSY: How dare you speak to me like this!

ROSS: You're being totally irresponsible.

ROSY: I am saving a young woman's life.

ROSS: A young woman who means nothing to you.

ROSY: Saving her from herself. She is vulnerable. As are all young women. Sometimes you have to look beyond your own tiny pool, and do what is right and necessary.

ROSS nods, cowed. He goes into his room and shuts the door.

BRIONY: Thank God for that.

ROSY: What?

BRIONY: There was I, thinking you two never argued. You're human after all.

ROSY: Shut up, Briony. And grab a couple of sticks, will you?

BRIONY takes two walking sticks from a large pot by the door and they exit. Beat. KEITH enters, bleary-eyed.

KEITH: What's all the…?

(He notices that CHARLES and SERENA's door is open and he peers inside.)

Hello?

(Returning, he looks puzzled.)

Bry? Briony?

He looks at ROSS and ROSY's door. He goes over and is about to knock but changes his mind. He then produces a baby's bottle which he puts into the microwave for thirty seconds, while he checks that the coast is clear. He takes the bottle out, shakes a couple of drops onto the back of his hand to make sure it's not too hot and then settles down to drink it. He's only had a sip when TABBY comes in. He hurriedly stows the bottle down the side of the armchair.

KEITH: Been out?

TABBY: What's that?

KEITH: What?

TABBY: That what you was hiding, bruv. I so saw you. I catched you, red-'anded. What is it?

KEITH: Nothing.

TABBY: I know about hiding shit. I spend my life doing it. What is it? Don't be embarrass. Is it gear?

KEITH: What?

TABBY: Gear.

KEITH: Gear?

TABBY: Drugs, man. Obviously it ain't then. Don't tell me you've got my skanky smalls. You dirty shit. You've nicked my panties.

KEITH: I haven't! Really, I haven't.

TABBY: Tell me then. If you ain't got no drugs and you ain't got no skankies, what you got?

KEITH: Milk.

TABBY: Milk?

KEITH: Milk, yes.

TABBY: For drinkin'?

KEITH: What other kind is there?

TABBY: You ain't got no milk.

KEITH: I have.

(He pulls out the bottle.)

See?

TABBY: That's a baby bottle. Oh.

KEITH: What?

TABBY: Nothing, cuz. Whatever gets you…

KEITH: It doesn't… I…wasn't…

TABBY: Whatever.

She gets into bed. She takes her clothes off and drops them onto the floor.

KEITH: My wife still feeds our son – and with us being away she's had to express it, otherwise her...

TABBY: Tits.

KEITH: They get very painful...so she pumps it out.

TABBY: And you drink it.

KEITH: No, well, I'm meant to pour it down the...but it's such a waste. Yes, I drink it. I drink my wife's breast milk. You probably think that's wrong.

TABBY: No such fing as wrong, babes. Live, that's all. Be who you wanna be.

Drink.

KEITH: I've sort of lost the... I might have it later.

TABBY: Your woman, she's a uptight girl and she's living in a uptight world.

KEITH: She's a bit depressed.

TABBY: Man, if ever saw a case for some serious sweets.

KEITH: She has...medication...but she won't take it. She's her own worst enemy. She's paralysed by the fear of fucking up and of course she fucks up all the time because...

TABBY: Because you keep climbing on top.

They both laugh.

KEITH: No, I mean it's a self-fulfilling prophecy. If only I could get on top once in a while.

(Pause.)

Goodnight.

TABBY: I love sex. It's the only fing that feels real. Drugs and shit, that's all right, but I've had it all and it don't interest me no more. I'll take it, yeah? But I don't live for it. Now sex, that's something else. Just fink about the millions of

66

bodies out there. Each one is a new kind of drug. You try it and move on. So many different kinds of body, bruv. I ain't being funny, right, but you and me we could have some together, if you still ain't getting none from your uptight girl. I don't mean here. In the city. I got a place. Fink about it, yeah? Give you my number. No strings. Just sex.

Pause.

KEITH: I couldn't.

TABBY: Fink about it.

KEITH: Oh, I already have.

TABBY: No strings.

KEITH: Still, I couldn't.

TABBY: That's cool. I'm going to sleep.

KEITH: Me too. *(Pause.)* Sorry. And thanks. If things were different…if I was a bit younger. And single. You're very nice. *(Silence.)* 'Night then.

But TABBY is asleep. KEITH stands there, holding his milk bottle. He is about to go to his room when he hears a noise. ROSS's door opens. KEITH quickly puts the bottle under TABBY's sheet. ROSS enters.

ROSS: Keith.

KEITH: All right?

ROSS: What are you doing?

KEITH: Nothing.

ROSS: Nothing?

KEITH: No.

ROSS: You're doing something.

KEITH: No I'm not.

ROSS: It's three a.m.

KEITH: I heard voices.

ROSS: Why are you standing there?

KEITH: Where?

ROSS: Next to the girl's bed, Keith.

KEITH: Oh yes.

ROSS: Why are you standing there?

KEITH: No reason.

ROSS: Well move away then.

KEITH: Why?

ROSS: Why not?

KEITH: I was just making sure she was all right.

ROSS: She's out. Everyone's out.

KEITH: Not everyone.

ROSS: Everyone. They're all at the rave.

KEITH: She's not. She came back.

> *KEITH moves aside and ROSS can now see that TABBY's bed is not empty.*

ROSS: She asleep?

KEITH: I think so, yes. We were having a little chat.

ROSS: Chat?

KEITH: And then she fell asleep.

ROSS: A chat? What about? Injecting drugs? Did you discuss your favourite brand of needle? Or which aluminium foil she prefers to burn her crystal meth in? You can't have a chat with someone like her.

KEITH: She's all right.

ROSS: She's not all right. She's a WMD. Kids like that should be in a home, fenced in with razor-wire.

KEITH: How's the foot?

ROSS: Terrible. Yes, they've all gone raving. Stark bloody raving. God help Charles and Serena. I just don't see the point in trying to control things that are beyond your control. You're still standing by her bed, Keith. Move away.

KEITH: Why?

ROSS: It looks pervy. Just move away.

KEITH: All right.

KEITH moves a little bit away from the bed.

ROSS: Right away.

KEITH: I don't know why you're...

ROSS: Just get away from the bed. Christ!

KEITH: Sorry.

ROSS: Sometimes you really irritate me, you know that?

KEITH: No. No, I didn't know that.

ROSS: Well you do. You always have done.

KEITH: Oh.

ROSS: Just go back to bed. Go on.

KEITH: Yes.

ROSS: I'm just a bit...you know. The old foot.

KEITH: Maybe I should go out and find them.

ROSS: They got themselves into this. They can bloody well get themselves out. Go back to bed.

KEITH: Right.

But KEITH lingers, thinking about the bottle...

ROSS: Please go away.

(KEITH goes to his room and shuts the door. ROSS pours a whisky and necks it. He pours himself another and sits in a chair, contemplating the sleeping TABBY.)

Fucking little bitch.

He swigs back his drink and stands up. He moves to the bed and looks down contemptuously at TABBY. He finds the bottle hidden by TABBY's feet. He then lifts the sheet and looks at her naked legs. He stands there for quite a while, staring. BRIONY enters, unseen by ROSS. He leans down and licks TABBY's leg. Then he replaces the sheet. He turns and sees BRIONY. They are frozen for a moment in

69

terrible recognition of what just happened. BRIONY moves into the room. ROSS starts to walk towards his room.

BRIONY: Rosy's bitten Charles. On the ear. We met them at the top of the field, by the stile, where the path leads down to the...we interrupted them. They were...you know? Rosy told Serena to put her clothes back on and stop behaving like a teenager. Serena said she couldn't put her clothes back on because her hands and feet were tied to the stile. Serena started laughing – a lot – and then Charles offered Rosy a tab of ecstasy. And that's when Rosy began screaming at them, screaming, and when Charles tried to restrain her she bit him. There's loads of blood. I need scissors. Keith!

She goes to her room. ROSS puts the lid on the whisky and puts it back on the shelf. He waits outside BRIONY's door for a moment as if intending to speak to her, but reconsiders, and goes towards his own room. BRIONY re-enters, followed by a bleary-eyed KEITH, hurriedly putting on a jumper. ROSS hovers. BRIONY goes into CHARLES and SERENA's room, speaking as she goes:

KEITH: I don't understand.

BRIONY: Look in the kitchen drawer.

KEITH: Why do you want scissors?

BRIONY: *(Off.)* Because I can't undo the knots.

KEITH: What knots?

BRIONY: *(Off.)* He tied them too tight.

KEITH: Who did?

BRIONY: *(Off.)* Just put your boots on, will you?

KEITH: What are you doing in their room?

BRIONY re-enters, carrying SERENA's medical bag.

BRIONY: She'll have some scissors in here. Come on. Quickly.

ROSS: Briony?

KEITH: I'm coming.

ROSS: Briony?

BRIONY: Hurry Keith! Quickly!

BRIONY exits. KEITH grabs his boots and heads out after her. ROSS stands, not knowing what to do. Fade to black.

SCENE TWO

The next morning. Very rainy outside. TABBY's bed is empty. SERENA, very hung-over, is making coffee alone in the kitchen. BRIONY comes out of her room. She is evidently in some discomfort.

BRIONY: Morning.

SERENA: I know.

BRIONY: Feeling bad?

(SERENA ignores her. BRIONY is looking around, searching for something.)

I can never sleep in. My brain won't let me. I don't suppose you've seen a…? Why would you? How's Charles? I hope his hearing's not affected. She was like a pit-bull. God knows what time she came back. If she even did come back. Maybe she's still out there, searching. And meanwhile the girl was safe and sound in bed. Oh, my boobs are killing me. Have you seen a…?

SERENA: What?

BRIONY: A bottle. Part of my breast pump.

SERENA: Sorry.

BRIONY: She's definitely got some issues. Rosy, I mean. Well, so has Tabby. But you see I thought Rosy was some kind of perfect person. They both hold stuff in, her and Ross, which isn't healthy, because one day the lid blows off, and innocent people get caught in the blast. The pressure just builds and builds. Like my boobs. Where is it? I can't express a thing without it.

SERENA: You seem to be doing all right so far.

BRIONY: I'll have to wake Keith. He had it last.

(She makes to go, but then turns…)

Did Charles ever…?

SERENA: What?

BRIONY: When you were breastfeeding…

SERENA: Yes, he did. If that's what you're asking. Voraciously. That's why our brats are so pale and spavined. They simply didn't get a look in. It's nothing to be ashamed of.

BRIONY: It confuses me. Milk is for babies and sex is for sex.

SERENA: Hogwash. Whatever keeps them interested. Chas and I are tirelessly creative in bed. I think I'm a kind of army assault course replacement for him. Ever tried tying him up?

BRIONY: Who, Keith?

SERENA: Chas loves it. All those years of soldiering. We take it in turns to play the prisoner. All good fun.

BRIONY: I'm not very good with pain.

SERENA: Pain's all right, as long as you don't take it too seriously.

BRIONY: I envy you. It must be lovely, not caring what other people think about you.

SERENA: I never think about it.

BRIONY: Rosy doesn't approve. Of the milk thing.

SERENA: You astound me.

BRIONY: In fact she thinks it's absolutely disgusting.

SERENA: Really? If I were you I'd declare the bottle lost and go and cheer the poor bloke up with a nice, warm double-shot latte.

BRIONY smiles embarrassedly. TABBY enters from CHARLES and SERENA's room. She is doing up her dress, and has a towel wrapped round her head.

BRIONY: Morning.

TABBY: Whassup?

BRIONY: Sorry?

TABBY: How's it?

BRIONY: Fine. Don't suppose you've seen a plastic baby bottle lying around?

TABBY: Nup.

SERENA: Go and see Keith. He'll help you out.

(BRIONY exits. TABBY quickly dries her hair and throws her things into a bag.)

You all right?

TABBY: Yeah.

SERENA: Don't have to go. Not now you've had a bath. Going straight back?

TABBY: Might do.

SERENA: Depends.

TABBY: Yeah.

SERENA: Come over and see us sometime. We're going to Antigua for half-term. You could come with.

TABBY: Don't know.

SERENA: Might all be dead in six weeks' time. If you're not though…? Sun and sand? Cocktails on the beach? Firebomb the embassy? Bit of a shitter things didn't work out with old what's-his-name. Don't tell me, traded you in for a younger model.

TABBY rummages in her bag and pulls out the baby bottle, still full of milk.

TABBY: Here.

SERENA: I won't ask. Drive recklessly.

TABBY: Fuck you.

SERENA: Fuck you too.

TABBY: Hey.

SERENA: What?

TABBY: Nuffin.

SERENA: See you.

(TABBY comes over and kisses SERENA, albeit very fleetingly. She exits. KEITH enters. SERENA hides the bottle.)

Morning.

KEITH: Hi.

SERENA: No double latte for you then.

KEITH: What?

SERENA: Coffee?

KEITH: If you've got some, yes. Where's your niece?

SERENA: Gone. Probably for the best.

(KEITH looks under the sofa-bed, feeling down the sides, checking under the sheet. SERENA pours KEITH a coffee.)

Lost something?

KEITH: Did she find a bottle?

SERENA: Bottle?

KEITH: A baby bottle. It may have somehow…found its way… into her bed.

SERENA: No. Nothing.

KEITH: Bloody hell.

ROSS enters.

ROSS: Morning.

KEITH: Morning.

ROSS: Morning, Serena. How's Charlie's ear?

SERENA: It's fine.

ROSS: Listen, I hope we can all draw a line under last night. Put it down to over-excitement. Showing off in front of our friends. That and too much booze. Can we? Serena?

SERENA: Of course.

ROSS: Good. Because Rosy certainly wants to heal the rift.

SERENA: There's no rift to heal. Honestly.

ROSS: She's never been one to hold a grudge.

SERENA: Right.

ROSS: What I'm saying is, there's no need for apologies.

SERENA: Oh good.

ROSS: Tabby's gone, has she?

SERENA: Yes.

ROSS: Perfect. Nice girl. Troubled, yes, but underneath all that…

SERENA: Coffee?

ROSS: I was going to make one for Rosy.

SERENA: Oh, let me do it. Really. It'd be my pleasure. How does she take it?

ROSS: Milky.

SERENA: Right. Sugar?

ROSS: No. Thank you, Serena.

SERENA: You're welcome to use our shower by the way. Terrific pressure.

ROSS: I might do that, actually.

SERENA: Do. Nip in before Chas nabs it.

ROSS: I will. *(Making to go.)* Thanks.

KEITH: You haven't seen a bottle anywhere?

ROSS: What sort of bottle?

KEITH: A baby bottle.

ROSS: Baby bottle?

KEITH: With milk in. It's part of Briony's breast pump. Have you seen it?

ROSS: What do you mean?

KEITH: What?

ROSS: Why would I have seen it?

KEITH: I just thought…

ROSS: What?

KEITH: You might have seen it.

ROSS: Where?

KEITH: I don't know. Did you?

ROSS: Did I what?

KEITH: Did you see it?

ROSS: When?

KEITH: Last night.

ROSS: What are you saying? What are you insinuating?

KEITH: Nothing. I think it might have been around here somewhere. Near the bed.

ROSS: Are you fucking with me, Keith?

KEITH: No, I'm only asking…

ROSS: What are you asking?

KEITH: I'm asking if you saw a baby bottle.

ROSS: Did I see a baby bottle? That's what you're asking me?

SERENA: Pretty simple question.

ROSS: I didn't see anything. All right?

KEITH: All right.

ROSS: Yes, well. So long as that's clear.

KEITH: Crystal clear.

ROSS: Good.

(ROSS heads for his room. BRIONY appears in her doorway.)

Morning.

BRIONY: Hello.

ROSS: How are we?

BRIONY: Um…well actually…

But ROSS has not waited for an answer. He has disappeared into his room.

SERENA: Keith, your other half needs you. Isn't that right, Briony? She's got something for you.

BRIONY looks embarrassed but motions for him to come in. He does so, and the door closes. SERENA now takes the baby bottle out and puts it into the microwave for thirty seconds. ROSS re-enters with a towel and a wash-bag. He crosses to CHARLES and SERENA's room.

ROSS: Sure you don't mind?

SERENA: Not in the slightest. We all have to share our toys.

He exits. She pours a cup of coffee and puts it on a tray. She now takes the milk and whizzes it in a jug to try and froth it. CHARLES appears in his dressing gown. One of his ears is bandaged.

CHARLES: There's someone in our bathroom.

SERENA: Ross. I said he could use the shower.

CHARLES: I need to shake the snake.

SERENA: You've got the whole of Wales at your disposal.

CHARLES: Pissing with rain. I'll use the sink.

CHARLES urinates in the kitchen sink. SERENA tries whizzing the milk again.

SERENA: Can't get it to froth.

CHARLES: What?

SERENA: It's not very frothy.

CHARLES: That's because I'm aiming at the side. If I shoot it straight at the plughole it's a different story.

SERENA: Give it one more go.

(She whizzes the milk again.)

Lower fat content than cow's. Surprising, really, given the amount of chocolate the woman eats. You still going?

CHARLES: Bloody good target practice. Bits of cornflake. I think that's a raisin. Die, you little bastard!

SERENA: There.

(She just finishes pouring the not-very-frothy milk into the coffee cup when ROSY enters, in her dressing gown.)

Perfect timing.

ROSY: Morning.

SERENA: Chas. He's a bit deaf in one ear. Chas!

CHARLES: What?

SERENA: Rosy is here.

CHARLES: Ah.

ROSY: Good morning.

CHARLES: Morning.

SERENA: Caught short, I'm afraid. Ross is in our shower. Chas, that's enough.

CHARLES: Can't stop halfway through. Got to finish the job. Every last insurgent. Flush the buggers into the Tigris. This is war.

SERENA: What can you do? He's having fun.

ROSY: Tabby's gone, I hear.

SERENA: Yes.

ROSY: Didn't put her bed away though, did she?

SERENA: I'll get Chas to do it.

ROSY: Nice girl. Troubled, yes, but...

SERENA: How was the rave?

ROSY: Not really my thing. Ross said you were making me some coffee.

SERENA: And so I have.

ROSY: Thank you, Serena. That means a lot to me.

SERENA: It's just a cup of coffee.

ROSY: No. It's more than that. It has meaning.

SERENA: Does it?

ROSY: It's an olive branch. You didn't need to, and yet you did. You proffer, and gratefully I accept. And now there is no need for any more discussion. We move on. Oh, you even frothed the milk.

SERENA: Natch.

ROSY: Thank you.

(She takes the coffee and drinks. SERENA smiles. CHARLES finishes at the sink.)

Did you sweeten it?

SERENA: No.

ROSY: It's quite sweet.

SERENA: Is it?

ROSY: I never have sugar in coffee.

SERENA: Maybe I did put some in by mistake. Sorry.

ROSY: Well, it won't kill me, will it? It's actually delicious.

SERENA: Oh good.

CHARLES helps himself to coffee.

ROSY: Really delicious. There's some interesting flavour in there. Can't quite put my finger on it.

SERENA: Really?

ROSY: Something under the surface.

SERENA: Chocolaty undertones? Slight bitterness? Some fruity top-notes. Melons maybe? Coconuts? Something a little bit winy…or Briony?

ROSY: Briony?

SERENA: Briny. Like the sea. It's Costa Rican. They have plantations on the coast.

CHARLES: Any more hot milk?

SERENA: Sorry darling, no. Not if Keith's got anything to do with it.

CHARLES: He hasn't.

SERENA: Oh, well then.

CHARLES: I'll have it cold.

SERENA: Good boy. He's really not hearing too well.

CHARLES gets the milk out of the fridge.

ROSY: There is something briny about it. It's organic, I know that.

SERENA: So is the milk.

ROSY: I'll put Tabby's bed away.

SERENA: Chas'll do it.

ROSY: No. I insist.

ROSY begins to fold away the sofa-bed. ROSS re-enters, a towel around his waist. His foot is still bandaged. CHARLES puts a piece of bread in the toaster.

CHARLES: How was the shower?

ROSS: Good. I stuck my foot out the side to keep the bandages dry.

ROSY: Clever thing.

ROSS: I'll just put some clothes on. Everything all right?

ROSY: Serena's made me the most delicious cup of coffee I think I've ever had.

SERENA: We're putting last night behind us. We're chockfull of bonhomie. Full of the milk of human kindness.

ROSY: That rhymed!

SERENA: I'll go and put some clothes on too. Chas?

CHARLES: I just put a bit of toast in.

ROSS: I think you mean bread.

ROSY: There. All tidied away! Serena?

SERENA: Mmm?

ROSY: The bed. All tidied away.

SERENA: Thanks.

ROSY: Pleasure. Maybe I'll get dressed too.

ROSS: Yes. *(Kisses her.)* And then we'll make a plan for the rest of the day.

ROSY: We have one already. We did it in the car on the way down.

ROSS: Oh yes.

ROSY: Thanks for the coffee. I might get you to make me another one later!

ROSS and ROSY go to their room. SERENA picks up the empty baby bottle.

SERENA: Could be tricky.

(SERENA rinses the bottle. She goes up to CHARLES and snogs him sexily.)

Don't be long. I'm very hung-over.

CHARLES: Fantastic.

SERENA: What are you going to have on your toast?

CHARLES: Butter and marmite.

SERENA: Remember to eat your crusts.

(SERENA goes towards their room.)

Really, really hung-over.

CHARLES: Fucking hell.

She goes into her room, closing the door behind her. CHARLES finishes his coffee. His toast pops up. He takes it out and begins buttering it in haste. There is the noise of glass smashing outside. He thinks of going to see what it is, but decides to finish spreading Marmite on his toast first. He then eats the toast, first steadily, then more hurriedly. He shoves the last bit in his mouth and, deciding to ignore the noise of the glass outside, proceeds towards the bedroom. There is a knock at the door. CHARLES turns, and reluctantly goes to open it. MR. MORGAN stands in the doorway, pointing CHARLES's gun at him.

MORGAN: Put your hands up please.

CHARLES: That's my gun.

MORGAN: Hands up please. And step back into the room.

CHARLES does as he's told.

CHARLES: You smashed my car window.

MORGAN: Sit down.

CHARLES: It wasn't even locked!

MORGAN: Sit down.

CHARLES: Now listen here. My wife's got a filthy hangover, and she gets jolly frisky when she's hung over and a chap doesn't want to miss out. I've always liked the Welsh. Bloody good singers. And I never gave much credit to all that guff about doing it with sheep. Anyway, this is dairy, isn't it? Is she a goer, your wife?

MORGAN: I'm a widower.

CHARLES: Possibly not then.

MORGAN: Where is the young girl?

CHARLES: God knows. What's this about?

MORGAN: Some Christian retreat this is.

CHARLES: What?

MORGAN: Where's Ross?

CHARLES: Getting dressed.

MORGAN: Ask him out here please. Now.

CHARLES knocks on ROSS and ROSY's door.

ROSY: *(Off.)* Who is it?

CHARLES: There's a chap here to see Ross. Looks like a farmer to me.

ROSY: Can he come back a bit later?

CHARLES: I'll ask him. Can you come back a bit later?

(MORGAN cocks the gun.)

I don't think he can. He's got my gun, you see.

Pause. The door opens a bit. ROSS speaks from somewhere behind it.

ROSS: Hello?

MORGAN: Come out here please.

ROSS: Why?

MORGAN: Come out here please.

ROSS: We're a bit busy at the moment.

MORGAN: Come out here please!

Pause. ROSS appears, followed by ROSY.

ROSS: What's this all about?

ROSY: Oh my God!

MORGAN: Where's the girl?

ROSS: Which girl?

CHARLES: Tabby.

ROSY: She left about half an hour ago.

CHARLES: Look, if you don't mind, I might just…

MORGAN: Stay where you are.

ROSY: Can you put the gun down please?

ROSS: She's gone back to London, thank the Lord. We did what we could for her, but she's a troubled soul. We were actually just saying a prayer for her.

MORGAN: This is not a Christian gathering. There is great sin amongst you.

ROSY: Please, Mr…?

ROSS: Morgan. Huw. I don't think we've done the introductions. This is my wife, Rosy.

ROSY: Hello Huw.

ROSS: And this is Charles.

CHARLES: Hi.

ROSS: Charles is married to Serena, who's in there.

CHARLES: She certainly is.

ROSY: He used to be in the SAS.

ROSS: Rosy.

ROSY: Well, he did. He's a trained killer. He's killed all sorts of people. How many people would you say you've actually killed?

CHARLES: Don't know, really.

ROSS: They're not meant to talk about it.

ROSY: Hundreds, though, probably. The point is, Mr. Morgan, he could break you in half.

SERENA appears, in her dressing gown.

SERENA: What the fuck's going on?

CHARLES: Sorry darling.

ROSY: He could crush you with one hand. So put the bloody gun down.

ROSS: He's never going to put it down now, is he?

MORGAN: Be quiet.

SERENA: Who is this?

ROSS: It's the local farmer. Huw, this is Serena.

SERENA: Why the fuck's he got your gun, Charlie?

MORGAN: Be quiet! Who else is in the house?

ROSS: Just Keith and Briony.

MORGAN: Where are they? In there?

ROSS: Yes.

ROSY: What's this all about? What has Tabby done?

SERENA: Tabby?

ROSY: She's done something.

MORGAN: Get them out here please.

SERENA: I think they're busy.

MORGAN: You.

SERENA: Sunday morning ritual.

MORGAN: Get them out here please.

SERENA: Bit of a breakthrough for the poor sods. Leave them to it. They've been having trouble in that department…

ROSS: The praying department. The words flew up, but they just couldn't seem to get a signal.

MORGAN: Be quiet! No more about praying. This is a den of iniquity. The Devil is residing here.

ROSY: How dare you.

SERENA: There's nothing wrong with a bit of nooky.

ROSS: They're not having nooky.

SERENA: They bloody well are.

ROSS: They are in there on bended knee.

SERENA: Well, one of them might be.

MORGAN: Sin and debauchery.

SERENA: They are married, for Christ's sake.

ROSY: Actually I'm not sure they are.

SERENA: Oh really?

ROSY: Ross?

ROSS: What?

ROSY: Are they married? I don't think they hold with it.

ROSS: Of course they're married. We're all married. This is a good, God-fearing household. Please put the gun down, Mr. Morgan!

MORGAN: Get them out here, now.

ROSS: I really don't want to disturb them while they're at prayer.

MORGAN: They're not at prayer!

ROSS: Of course they are. As we were, until you interrupted us. We all were. Now will you please stop pointing that thing at my head!

MORGAN: You lied to me. You said this was a retreat for the purposes of prayer.

ROSS: It is.

MORGAN: It is not. It is a blasphemous sex orgy.

ROSS: No.

MORGAN: Yes.

ROSS: There are no sexual relations going on in this house at the moment.

MORGAN: You are a liar.

ROSS: No.

MORGAN: Yes! Yes!

Just at this moment, things begin building to a sudden and seemingly earth-shattering climax in KEITH and BRIONY's room...

BRIONY: *(Off.)* YES! YES! Oh my God! Oh my GOD! OH GOD! OH GOD! OH GOD! OH FUCK. FUCK! YES! FUCK! YES! YES! YES! OH JESUS! OH FUCKING JESUS! OH SWEET FUCKING JESUS! AAAAAAAAAAAAH! YES!!!!

Long pause.

SERENA: Well, they're certainly not Church of England.

MORGAN: Get them out here. NOW!

ROSS knocks on KEITH and BRIONY's door.

ROSS: Keith! Can you both come out here please? It's fairly urgent.

KEITH: *(Off.)* Hang on.

CHARLES: Lucky buggers.

ROSS: I'm sure they won't be long. Why don't we all sit down? I have an injured foot.

MORGAN nods.

ROSY: I could put the kettle on.

MORGAN: No.

The two couples sit down.

SERENA: So. How's farming these days?

MORGAN: Be quiet.

SERENA: Whatever my niece has done to upset you, which I can't imagine is very much…

ROSS: I'm sure Mr. Morgan will tell us.

ROSY: Did she vandalise your tractor or something?

SERENA: We'll write you a cheque, won't we, Charles?

CHARLES: As long as I get my gun back in one piece.

MORGAN: You are related to the girl?

SERENA: She's my sister's daughter, yes.

MORGAN: Then the blame falls squarely on you. Where is your sister?

SERENA: Committed suicide. Drug overdose. Shortly after my brother-in-law killed himself on his motorbike.

MORGAN: Then as I said, the blame falls on you.

SERENA: Oh fuck off. Who do you think you are?

MORGAN: I am my son's father.

SERENA: Congratulations.

MORGAN: My son is severely handicapped. He lost his mother when he was only six. I have struggled for ten years to provide a strong and loving framework for the boy. Keeping the light of hope alive in his heart, with the help of Our Lord. And he is a fine lad. Intelligent, happy enough in his way. Grateful to God, in spite of his unfortunate condition. And now, in one night, all my good work has been ruined.

BRIONY appears in the doorway of her room.

BRIONY: Oh!

ROSS: Briony, this is Mr. Morgan. He's just telling us about his poor son.

MORGAN: Where's your…partner?

CHARLES: He's just lowering the showerhead.

BRIONY: Why's he got a gun?

ROSY: Tabby's done something to his son.

BRIONY: What?

ROSY: He's just about to tell us.

ROSS: She must have broken into their house.

ROSY: She's stolen something.

SERENA: She wouldn't have hurt him. Whatever it was, I'm sure it wasn't deliberate.

MORGAN: How do you know?

SERENA: Because she's my niece.

MORGAN: You don't know what she did!

SERENA: Tell us then. For God's sake put us out of our misery.

MORGAN: She had sex with him!

Silence.

SERENA: Is that so bad?

CHARLES: Good on them, that's what I say.

SERENA: It's natural.

CHARLES: And good on you and Keith as well.

SERENA: A couple of youngsters, experimenting.

BRIONY: You didn't hear, did you?

SERENA: All part of growing up.

ROSS: When was this?

BRIONY: I'm so embarrassed.

SERENA: Don't be.

MORGAN: My son is severely disabled.

ROSS: Yes, we know.

CHARLES: Tabby is a bit of a bike. She started when she was about nine.

SERENA: Chas, shut up.

CHARLES: Right-o.

ROSY: How did you find out?

MORGAN: He told me everything. I went to his room to give the boy his breakfast. He was in tears. He could barely speak.

ROSS: Where did they do it? I mean, where did it take place?

ROSY: Ross.

ROSS: What?

ROSY: There's no need to be prurient.

ROSS: Or prudish. Just trying to establish the facts.

MORGAN: In his bedroom. He has a ground floor bedroom.

SERENA: Where were you?

MORGAN: Upstairs. Fast asleep. I took a couple of pills to help me sleep through the terrible noise.

CHARLES: *(To BRIONY.)* See? Not just you who makes a din.

MORGAN: Beg pardon?

CHARLES: A lot of the fillies I've known have loved a good yelp. The yelping actually helps them achieve liftoff.

ROSS: He's talking about the rave.

CHARLES: Is he? Oh.

ROSY: Who let her in then? Your boy?

MORGAN: She wanted to make a phone call. Long-distance, if you please. My son was up late, on his computer. Told her I was upstairs, dead to the world. She seized her chance to exploit his vulnerability.

ROSY: How is he now?

MORGAN: Deeply traumatised. I don't know if he'll ever recover.

SERENA: Oh what bollocks.

ROSY: Serena.

MORGAN: She raped him!

SERENA: No, I'm sorry. If the boy didn't want it, he wouldn't have got it. I'm assuming we're talking the whole hog here? Yes? Well, I'm a doctor so I know about bodies, and I'm telling you, Mr. Morgan, it wouldn't have happened without more than a little involvement from your son. You men going to back me up?

CHARLES: Absolutely.

SERENA: Ross?

ROSS: Yes, I suppose so.

SERENA: Now, he might be feeling aggrieved that my niece only wanted a one-night stand, but frankly it's better than nothing – they're not exactly lining up, are they? I bet he had a fabulous time, and the reason he told you was that he simply wanted you to know he's not quite so helpless and disabled as you like to portray him.

MORGAN: He was in tears!

SERENA: Tears of relief, probably.

CHARLES: Pure bloody joy, more like.

MORGAN: You don't know anything. You don't know my son, or me. All you know are your clever London ways and your clever London words.

SERENA: What I don't know is what you think you're going to gain by waving my husband's gun in the air. Now put it down, then go home to your son and ask him how it really was for him and stop putting silly words like rape into his mouth.

MORGAN: I could use this.

SERENA: Could you?

MORGAN: I could shoot any one of you and the world wouldn't be a bit worse off.

BRIONY: Serena's right. We can be very seduced by the idea of being a victim. I know I have been in the past. All our experiences, good or bad, can be opportunities for learning.

ROSS: Well said, Briony. Now give me the gun.

CHARLES: Yes, give him it. So I can give you a bloody good smack in the face.

SERENA: Charlie.

MORGAN: I won't take advice from you on how to bring up my child. Your generation couldn't give a damn about anything except yourselves.

SERENA: That's very unfair. I for one am very fond of shopping.

MORGAN: Don't mock me! Not one of you is serious enough to be a parent. You come here for a weekend of drink and debauchery. Where are your children?

ROSY: Our children are fine. We have an excellent au pair... well...

ROSS: They're with very close friends in Bristol.

SERENA: And ours are quite old enough to look after themselves. The oldest is four and a half now.

ROSS: Serena.

SERENA: London kids grow up so fast.

MORGAN: And as for you and your partner...

BRIONY: What?

KEITH appears on cue.

CHARLES: Talk of the devil. Look at him. Cat with the bloody cream!

MORGAN: Your name is Keith, is it?

KEITH: What's going on?

MORGAN: Poor little mite has to go to hospital and you choose to stay here copulating. It's unnatural.

ROSS: Right, let's wrap this up now, shall we?

KEITH: What are you talking about?

CHARLES: Oh come off it, old man. They could have heard you in Abergavenny.

KEITH: No, who's gone to hospital?

MORGAN: Your son. Don't pretend you don't know what I'm talking about.

KEITH: I don't. I haven't got a clue. Briony?

MORGAN: Or maybe your friend never told you. You decide not to trouble them in the end, did you? Their child in hospital.

BRIONY: Keith?

KEITH: Ross?

ROSS: Oh yes! It slipped my mind. Your mum phoned through to the farm.

BRIONY: Oh God.

KEITH: And he didn't bring the message?

MORGAN: Of course I did.

ROSS: He kicked the bedroom door.

MORGAN: He broke his toe.

BRIONY: No!

KEITH: Broke it?

BRIONY: Oh Jesus. Finn. My baby.

ROSS: It's just a toe. They didn't keep him in. I decided not to tell you.

CHARLES: Bloody hell.

KEITH: Why?

ROSS: For your own good. You needed this time away. It was important for you and Briony.

BRIONY: Keith.

KEITH: It's all right, love.

ROSS: And he's fine.

BRIONY: He's broken his toe.

KEITH: They took him to hospital and you didn't tell us?

ROSS: I checked. I rang your mum.

KEITH: When?

ROSS: I rang her yesterday and then again today. He's fine.

BRIONY: Is he?

ROSS: Absolutely fine.

KEITH: On what phone?

ROSS: What?

KEITH: On what phone?

MORGAN: Not on mine.

ROSS: No. On mine…on my…mobile.

KEITH: Your mobile?

ROSS: I managed to…get a signal…in the end.

KEITH: You bastard.

ROSY: He was doing you a favour. You're both such worriers.

KEITH: Oh, are we?

ROSY: You know you are. And that's what friends are for, to help you recognise your little shortcomings, and try to bring about some change. You've both been crying out for help.

ROSS: It's true. You tie yourselves in knots. Parenting is so much easier than you make it out to be.

ROSY: You needed taking in hand, and Ross was the only one who knew you well enough – and cared enough – to do it.

ROSS: It's called tough love.

ROSY: If anything, you should be very grateful. As you can see, Mr. Morgan, we've moved the conversation on. You needn't stay any longer.

ROSS: Yes, off you trot.

ROSY: I'll put the kettle on.

MORGAN: Don't you move!

BRIONY: Keith?

KEITH: Why's he got a gun?

BRIONY: I want to see my baby.

KEITH: You will.

BRIONY: I don't want to die.

MORGAN: *(To KEITH.)* Sit down, all of you!

ROSS: Oh for heaven's sake.

MORGAN: Sit!

KEITH obeys.

ROSY: Now look. You're obviously not going to shoot anyone, so just give us the gun.

MORGAN: We're all staying exactly where we are.

ROSY: In a minute one of us will get extremely bored of this and stand up. What will you do then?

MORGAN: I'll shoot you if I have to.

ROSY: Of course you won't.

MORGAN: *(Shouting.)* YOU DON'T KNOW WHAT I'M CAPABLE OF!

ROSY: Fine. We'll all sit here and wait for you to work out what it is exactly that you want.

MORGAN: I know what I want.

ROSS: What then? What is it?

MORGAN: I want an apology.

ROSY: From whom?

SERENA: From us of course. From everyone. Okay. I'm terribly sorry for what Tabby's done. Dirty little slut. We're both really, really sorry.

CHARLES: Yes, we are.

SERENA: Poor little chap. I really hope he's not too miz. Honestly, we're very sorry.

ROSY: Enough?

MORGAN: No. All of you.

ROSY: What?

MORGAN: An apology from all of you.

ROSY: Oh come off it.

KEITH: I'm fine with that. I'm sorry Mr. Morgan. Aren't you, Briony?

BRIONY: Yes, I am.

KEITH: We're really sorry we came. Really sorry we brought all this trouble down here. I hope you can forgive us. And thanks for bringing the message about Finn.

BRIONY: I hope your son is okay.

MORGAN: I hope so too.

ROSY: Well don't look at me. I had nothing to do with it.

SERENA: Oh come off it, Rosy.

ROSY: I have spent the entire weekend mothering you all. A weekend that was meant, ironically enough, to be free of children. And yet when push came to shove who was the only one prepared to be a responsible adult? Who went out scouring the hillsides for that damned girl at two in the morning while her relations, who should have done it, were themselves behaving like delinquent teenagers? I did. I am not accepting any blame for what she did.

ROSS: Me neither. I have nothing to apologise for.

BRIONY: Don't you?

ROSY: No, he doesn't. We're blameless. We didn't even invite her.

BRIONY: I bet you can think of something, Ross.

ROSS stares at BRIONY.

ROSY: We organised the whole damn weekend. We bought the food and the wine. There's absolutely nothing for us to feel bad about.

BRIONY: Ross?

ROSS: No. Nothing.

KEITH: Apart from not telling us about Finn. Apart from lying about your phone not having a signal.

ROSY: Well, I'm sure he's sorry about that, but as I said he was doing it for your own good.

KEITH: Are you sorry about that?

ROSS: Yes, of course. I'm sorry. I apologise to you both.

SERENA: There we go. Not so difficult, is it?

BRIONY: More. There's more you can say sorry for.

ROSS: Is there?

BRIONY: Look into your heart.

ROSY: I don't know what you're talking about.

BRIONY: There's always more we can feel bad about, if we look.

ROSS: Okay, I invited Charles and Serena. And if I hadn't, Tabby would never have come. Mr. Morgan's son wouldn't have lost his cherry, Charles wouldn't have lost half an ear. And I wouldn't have got a fucking kitchen knife in the foot either. So yes, I'm sorry for that. I'm sorry, Charles. I'm sorry, Mr. Morgan.

SERENA: There now.

ROSS: Happy now?

BRIONY: No.

KEITH: Briony?

BRIONY: Go further, Ross. Get it all out on the table.

ROSY: He's apologised, hasn't he? What do you want from him?

BRIONY: Come on, Ross. You can do it.

ROSY: What's she talking about?

BRIONY: Ross? What am I talking about?

ROSS: All right. I apologise for everything. The things I did, and the things I thought of doing but didn't. I even apologise for the things I didn't think of doing. I apologise for it all. I'm a terrible person. Okay? I'm controlling, and I'm conceited, and I'm a hypocrite. I'm two-faced, and smug, and I'm not a very good friend and I'm probably an awful dad and I know I could be a better husband.

ROSY: No.

ROSS: Yes. I could be a better husband. Much, much better. But I'm just another fucked-up human being. Are you satisfied, Briony?

SERENA: You need counselling.

ROSS: Are you satisfied?

ROSY: What's going on?

ROSS: Are you satisfied?!

ROSY: What's going on here?

ROSS: Nothing.

ROSY: Obviously something's going on. Briony?

BRIONY: What?

ROSY: You know something.

BRIONY: No, I don't.

ROSY: Something about Ross.

ROSS: No, she doesn't.

ROSY: I'm not an idiot. What do you know, Briony? Tell me!

BRIONY: There's nothing to tell.

ROSY: Don't make me cross. If it's to do with my husband then you have a duty to tell me.

BRIONY: No, I don't.

ROSY: There is something then?

BRIONY: It's between me and Ross.

ROSY: A secret?

BRIONY: Yes.

ROSS: Jesus.

ROSY: Sorry?

ROSS: Nothing.

ROSY: Why did you say that?

ROSS: Can we move on?

ROSY: No. There's something that Briony feels you need to
apologise for, Ross. Something of a personal nature?

ROSS: I haven't got a clue.

ROSY: You must do.

ROSS: I haven't got a clue!

ROSY: Briony? I'm talking to you, Briony.

SERENA: Let it go, Rosy.

ROSY: You keep your big nose out of it. I'm asking you a
question. Have the decency to answer it.

BRIONY: It's private.

ROSY: There's no such thing as private! Ross and I are
married.

BRIONY: Ask him then. I'm not saying another word about it.

ROSY: Tell me, Briony! TELL ME!

BRIONY: No.

ROSY: You little bitch.

BRIONY: What did you call me?

KEITH: Did you just call her a bitch?

ROSS: Rosy.

ROSY: Shut up, Ross.

ROSS: You're making a spectacle of yourself.

ROSY: No, I'm not. I'm simply doing what any woman in
my position would do when something shadowy emerges
about her husband's conduct.

ROSS: Shadowy?

ROSY: Obviously it's shadowy or why would our neurotic
friend there be keeping it from us all?

BRIONY: Neurotic now? Neurotic bitch.

ROSY: I will not be kept in the dark by a pathetic worm like her!

ROSS: You're being totally out of order. Just calm down.

ROSY: *(Standing.)* I will not calm down!

MORGAN: Sit down!

ROSY: And I will not sit down either!

ROSS: Sit down, Rosy.

ROSY: I will NOT SIT DOWN!

MORGAN: Sit down or I'll shoot!

ROSY: Shoot me then! Go on, you Welsh git!

BRIONY suddenly pulls ROSY down onto the sofa.

BRIONY: Sit down!

ROSY is stunned that BRIONY did this. Beat. Then…

ROSY: Aaaaarrrrgggghhhh!

…as ROSY turns and jumps on top of BRIONY, who screams.

BRIONY: Get her off!

KEITH then tries to pull ROSY off but is dealt a blow to the head for his efforts.

ROSY: Fuck you! *(To BRIONY.)* You bloody cow!

ROSS: For God's sake!

BRIONY: Help me!

ROSS: Control yourself!

CHARLES: She can't.

ROSY: What do you know?

CHARLES: Take her in hand, old man.

BRIONY: Ask Ross!

ROSY: I'm not asking Ross, I'm asking you!

BRIONY: Ross!

ROSY: Tell me, damn you! What do you know?

BRIONY: Ross, tell her!

SERENA: Yes, tell her, will you? Anything to shut her up.

ROSY: Fuck off, Serena.

SERENA: Charming.

CHARLES: Tell her, old man. It's the only way.

ROSY: You all know. They all know. You bastard.

CHARLES: No, actually, I don't know…

ROSY: What is it, Ross? What is it that everyone knows?

SERENA: Neither do I.

ROSY: What is it!! Tell me, Ross!! FUCKING TELL ME!!

ROSS: All right. I licked her.

Moment.

ROSY: What?

ROSS: I licked her. Licked her leg.

ROSY: Whose leg?

ROSS: Tabby's.

ROSY: You licked her?

ROSS: Yes.

ROSY: You licked Tabby's leg?

ROSS: I licked her shin. Her left shin.

ROSY: She's seventeen.

ROSS: She was asleep.

ROSY: You're disgusting.

CHARLES: She wouldn't have minded.

MORGAN: I knew it. There are words for people like you.

ROSY: You licked a teenager's shin? I don't know what to say.

MORGAN: The police should be informed. He's a bloody paedophile.

ROSS: I didn't…do anything else. Did I, Briony?

ROSY: Oh God.

ROSS: Did I?

ROSY: Of course you did. Obviously you did.

ROSS: No Rosy…

ROSY: You fucked the nanny. You fucked Yelena, didn't you? *(Silence.)* Of course you did. Of course you fucked her. Well, you'd better start thinking about where you're going to be when we get back to London, because I'm not having you in my house. I'm not having you kiss my children. *(Indicating CHARLES and SERENA.)* Perhaps some of your more sexually enlightened friends could take you in. You could kiss some of theirs. They might even like to watch.

KEITH: Well, Mr. Morgan, as you can see we don't really need you here. We're doing a pretty good job of destroying ourselves.

CHARLES: Yes, bugger off now, will you?

SERENA: But Rosy hasn't said sorry.

KEITH: I think we'll just…

SERENA: We all, as a group, owe Mr. Morgan an apology, and everyone has done it apart from you, Rosy.

ROSS: There's really nothing she has to apologise for. Not to him anyway. I think you should go now.

SERENA: I disagree. Come on, Rosy. There must be something.

CHARLES: Just one little word. Then he'll sod off.

SERENA: That's right, isn't it, Huw? One tiny word and you'll leave.

ROSY: You can all fuck off. I am the only decent person in this room. I owe no one an apology.

SERENA: Actually you do. See, poor Mr. Morgan, being a Christian, just had his earlier trauma multiplied many times over by having to endure the sounds of unbridled fornication between an unmarried couple. That would never have happened if Keith here hadn't pounced on

Briony for his daily fix of milk, which of course was all your fault.

CHARLES: Why?

SERENA: Because he wouldn't have needed booby if you, greedy madam, hadn't drunk his secret stash of mummy juice in your perfect café latte.

(Pause. ROSY stares at SERENA, who smiles at her.)

So in fact it was Briony who's been mothering you.

ROSY suddenly stands up. She vomits on ROSS.

MORGAN: Sit down!

ROSY rushes towards the bedroom, but MR. MORGAN is in the way, and he tries to bar her way.

ROSY: Get out of my way!

ROSS: *(Standing up.)* Let her go!

MORGAN: I said sit down!

ROSY pushes past him. Suddenly the gun goes off. BRIONY screams. ROSY runs to the bathroom. ROSS drops to his knees in agony.

ROSS: Shit!

MR. MORGAN drops the gun and, panicking, shuffles towards the front door.

KEITH: Jesus.

CHARLES picks up the gun.

CHARLES: Right.

SERENA: Charles!

CHARLES: Stay where you are!

ROSS: Fuck!

SERENA: Where did he get you?

ROSS: My fucking leg. Aaaaah!

MORGAN looks back.

CHARLES: Bastard.

SERENA: Let him go.

CHARLES: But…

SERENA: Just let him go, Chas.

ROSS: Aaaah! Oh my sweet God!

(MORGAN has gone.)

Fucking hell! Aaaaaaah.

SERENA: I'll get my bag.

CHARLES: I won't kill him. I'll just pepper his arse.

SERENA: *(Firmly.)* No. Stay!

SERENA goes to her room.

CHARLES: If it's any help, the first time I took a bullet I shat myself. Northern Ireland. I had had a filthy curry the night before though. How are the bowels?

ROSS: *(Suddenly recovering.)* Fine. Has he gone?

CHARLES: Oh, well done. That's very good.

ROSS: He won't be coming back in a hurry.

KEITH: Excuse me.

BRIONY: Where are you going?

KEITH: To pack.

KEITH exits to their bedroom.

CHARLES: Hook, line and bloody sinker.

ROSS: Time for a drink, I reckon.

CHARLES: He was faking it!

SERENA has returned with her First Aid kit. ROSS pours himself a whisky.

SERENA: What?

CHARLES: He's okay. Faked the whole thing.

SERENA: Well, he's not in PR for nothing.

CHARLES: I knew a chap who shot his own bollocks off. Tragic.

ROSS: By mistake?

CHARLES: No. Hated being male.

SERENA: It's a curse. I feel very sorry for you chaps. Ruled by the tyrant testosterone. But there are some benefits to a fine pair of goolies.

CHARLES: She loves my goolies. She's even got names for them.

ROSS: Too much information?

CHARLES: Bismarck and Rodney. Famous battleships. Packed full of seamen.

BRIONY laughs hysterically. CHARLES and SERENA join in. It's CHARLES's oldest gag. ROSS smiles, trying his best to enjoy the moment.

SERENA: Come round and see us sometime. Seriously. We'd like it, wouldn't we?

CHARLES: We'd have a laugh.

SERENA: We really would. You can take life too seriously, I reckon.

BRIONY: Okay then. Yes. We'd love to.

(KEITH has appeared, their clothes stuffed into a bag.)

Wouldn't we?

KEITH: What?

BRIONY: Go round to theirs sometime.

KEITH: That would be really nice, yes.

ROSS: Tell you what. Why don't you all come for dinner round at ours next Saturday?

CHARLES: Who wants a drink?

SERENA: Vodka please. And make it a stiff one.

CHARLES: Not going to spoil your hangover, is it?

SERENA: Not a jot.

CHARLES: Keith?

KEITH: Better not.

CHARLES: Oh yes. Driving.

KEITH: No, I just had a double load of milk.

(They laugh.)

(To BRIONY.) Come on.

ROSS: You're not really going?

KEITH: Say goodbye to Rosy for us. And no hard feelings, yeah?

ROSS: Really?

KEITH: My partner and I don't hold grudges. Do we, Briony?

BRIONY: Don't we?

KEITH: No we don't.

ROSS: Good. I'm glad.

KEITH: But this is from Finn…

KEITH stamps very hard on ROSS's foot. BRIONY is shocked and at the same time slightly thrilled. ROSS goes down immediately, doubled up with pain.

ROSS: Aaaaaaaaaaaaaaaah!

KEITH: Who does. Bye.

CHARLES: Bye.

SERENA: Bye.

KEITH and BRIONY leave.

ROSS: He's broken my fucking toe.

SERENA: How appropriate.

ROSS: The fucking little…!

SERENA: Any more swearing and you'll go straight to bed with no fucking tea.

CHARLES finds this hilarious.

CHARLES: No fucking tea! Ha ha ha!

SERENA: More voddy! More voddy!

ROSS: Help me! For God's sake! My toe! Serena!

SERENA: What's the magic word?

ROSS: Please. Please help me. I beg you! Please!

SERENA: Oh very well.

SERENA reaches for her FIRST AID bag, but CHARLES takes it off her. He is cross.

CHARLES: No! I'm sorry, but actually it's not.

SERENA: What?

CHARLES: The magic word. It's not 'please'. Not at the moment. I've been pretty bloody patient but there's only so much a chap can take. Right now, actually, if you want to know, the magic word is rumpy-pumpy! Catch!

He throws the medical bag hard to ROSS who catches it badly.

SERENA: Oh Charles! Are you very cross?

CHARLES: Yes I bloody well am.

SERENA: Have I been awfully bad?

CHARLES: You damn well have. I've a good mind to put you on the naughty step.

SERENA: Oh Chas, yes, do it! Put me on it, Chas. I love the naughty step. Put me on the naughty step now!

He sweeps SERENA off her feet and into their bedroom. At that moment ROSY appears in her bedroom doorway, looking terrible. She watches ROSS writhing in pain as the lights fade to black.

WWW.OBERONBOOKS.COM